I0753325

INTEGRATING THE INTENSIVE METHOD™

The Proven How-To Guide for
Designing and Delivering High-Impact
Intensives — and Building a Profitable,
Sustainable Practice with Confidence

CRISTINA MARIE WEHNER
MTSC, LCMHCS, CSAT-S, CPTT-S, CCBRT, CMAT, CHFP

Integrating The Intensive Method™: The Proven How-To Guide for Designing and Delivering High-Impact Intensives — and Building a Profitable, Sustainable Practice with Confidence by Cristina Maria Wehner

First printing, 2026

ISBN: 979-8-9946625-0-2
Library of Congress Case Number: 2026909665

Cristina Marie Wehner
21345 Catawba Avenue
Cornelius, NC 28031

www.theintensivemethod.com

Printed in the United States of America

Praise for *Integrating The Intensive Method™*

"Wow!" That was my first reaction when reading this book. Cristina Wehner has written the seminal work on intensives. Follow her direction and watch your practice transform. She has a gift for making what initially looks complicated into an easy to follow guide that will allow you to make unprecedented progress with your clients. Her passion for this work flows from every page.

Dr. Milton S. Magness
Author of Stop Sex Addiction, Thirty Days to Hope and Freedom, and others

Tina's work is nothing short of powerful and deeply needed. Integrating The Intensive Method is a masterfully written guide that brings clarity, integrity, and intentionality to a model of care that has the capacity to truly transform lives. Tina has a rare gift—she doesn't just teach a method, she shepherds hearts. Her passion for healing, restoration, and truth is evident on every page.

This work thoughtfully exposes the schemes that often keep individuals and relationships bound, while offering a pathway toward freedom, wholeness, and sustainable change. Whether relationships are restored collectively or healing must first happen individually, Tina honors the process with wisdom, compassion, and unwavering ethical grounding. Her impact on countless lives—clinicians and clients alike—is a testament to her calling and commitment to this work. This book is a gift to the helping profession and a roadmap for healing done the right way.

Tamela Davis, Co-founder of the Devoted Dreamers Foundation,
Life Coach, and Founder of "The F Word"

Table of Contents

Acknowledgments 9

PART 1 — Understanding The Intensive Method **11**

Chapter 1 The Call to Practice Differently 13
Chapter 2 The Promise of Intensives 20
Chapter 3 Ethical Considerations and Boundaries 27
Chapter 4 The Anatomy of an Intensive 33

PART 2 — Building and Marketing Your Intensive **45**

Chapter 5 Your Ideal Client & How to Reach Them 47
Chapter 6 Marketing The Intensive Method 53
Chapter 7 Developing Your Brand Identity 61
Chapter 8 Shaping Your Comprehensive Marketing Plan 70
Chapter 9 Packaging, Pricing, and Profit 76

PART 3 — Delivering Effective Intensives **87**

Chapter 10 Designing the 3-Day Experience 89
Chapter 11 Therapeutic Tools and Modalities 96
Chapter 12 Experiential and Expressive Therapy Options 103
Chapter 13 Addressing Trauma and Crisis 110

PART 4 — Preparing You and Your Clients for Success **117**

Chapter 14 Screening Clients for Fit 119
Chapter 15 Assessment and Intake for Successful Intensives 126
Chapter 16 Treatment Planning that Works 133

PART 5 — Optimizing the Intensive Practitioner's Life **141**

Chapter 17 Time Management and Your Work Week 143
Chapter 18 Self-Care as a Clinical Competency 153
Chapter 19 Business Infrastructure and Tools 162
Chapter 20 Developing Client Resources and Workbooks 167

PART 6 — Elevating Client Outcomes **175**

Chapter 21 Building Trust and Safety Fast 177
Chapter 22 Engaging Resistance and Ambivalence 183
Chapter 23 Empowering Clients As Collaborators 189

Chapter 24	Rigorous Aftercare and Sustained Success	197
Chapter 25	Client and Clinician Evaluation Tools	201
Chapter 26	Taking the Leap: Mindset Shifts for Clinicians	209
PART 7 — Expand Your Intensive Revenue Streams		**213**
Chapter 27	Creating Intensive Therapy Products to Expand Revenue Streams	215
Chapter 28	Offering Onsite Accommodations	223
Chapter 29	Scaling Your Practice	227
Chapter 30	Innovations for Revenue Growth	232
PART 8 — The Long Game		**237**
Chapter 31	Professional Growth and Supervision	239
Chapter 32	Leadership and Team Building	245
Chapter 33	Continuing Education and Specialization	251
Chapter 34	Creative Expansion and Flexibility	256
Chapter 35	Conclusion: Building a Life and Business You Love	262

Acknowledgements

This book did not begin with a manuscript.

It began with people.

It began with clients who trusted me with their stories, their pain, their courage, and their hope—often at moments when everything felt uncertain. While the details of their stories are protected, the wisdom they offered me through their honesty shaped every page of this book. You taught me what actually works in the room, what breaks open real change, and what happens when we slow down enough to do deep work well. I carry your resilience with me always.

I am deeply grateful to the clinicians, coaches, and helping professionals who have walked alongside me over the years—those who challenged my thinking, sharpened my skills, and reminded me that good therapy is both an art and a discipline.

I want to acknowledge Dr. Milton Magness, whose pioneering work with the 3-Day Intensive served as the master model and catalyst that taught me what intensive work could truly be. His brilliance, generosity, and leadership shaped not only my clinical approach, but my confidence that deep, focused work can transform lives.

I am also profoundly thankful for my state supervisors, Lynn and Jill, who believed in me early—offering guidance, encouragement, and steady support at a time when I was still finding my footing as a clinician. Your belief helped me begin to believe in myself.

This work would not exist without the colleagues and collaborators who helped shape it from an idea into something tangible.

I am especially grateful to my original team at LivingWell—professionals who linked arms with me and helped build something meaningful together. Monica, Christi, and Kris: your teamwork, courage, and commitment during those early years mattered more than you know.

And to my current team of absolute rockstars—especially Sarah, whose steadiness, competence, and behind-the-scenes leadership somehow keeps the world in orbit—this work is stronger because of you.

I am especially thankful for the therapists and practitioners who were willing to experiment—to try something different, to step outside traditional models, and to trust that intensive work could serve both clients and clinicians more fully. Your questions, feedback, and real-world application helped refine this method into something practical, ethical, and sustainable.

To my friend Hope—thank you for the iron-sharpening-iron friendship that pushes us both to lead with excellence, integrity, and courage. I am better because of you.

To my family: thank you for your grace, your flexibility, and your steady presence. This work required time, focus, and energy, and you made room for all of it.

I am grateful for the men who encouraged my growth, challenged me to become stronger, and affirmed my capacity to lead with integrity, wisdom, and courage as a woman—especially my stepdad, who will forever be my hero and model of leadership; and to the bosses who took risks on me and believed in my potential—Jim, Farrell, and Greg—thank you for supporting my dreams before they were fully formed.

To my mom, who has always stood by my side; to my cousin Adam, who has always felt more like a brother; and to my three children—my greatest blessings and the truest joy of my life—everything I do is better because of you.

Finally, I want to acknowledge the deeper calling behind this work. This book reflects years of listening—to clients, to colleagues, to my own limitations, and to the quiet nudges that kept saying there was a better way to do this work. The Intensive Method is not about doing more. It is about doing what matters—carefully, intentionally, and with respect for the humanity of everyone involved.

Portions of this book were developed with the assistance of AI tools, including OpenAI's ChatGPT, which supported the author in drafting, editing, and refining content. All final interpretations, edits, and conclusions are the author's own.

PART 1

Understanding The Intensive Method

CHAPTER 1

The Call to Practice Differently

In an age of increasing virtualization, the landscape of therapy and life coaching is evolving dramatically. More and more people are seeking mental health care, and exponentially more of them are finding help and support via apps, telehealth, and virtual appointments.

While there is much to celebrate in this season—not the least of which is the receding tide of stigmatism surrounding mental health—this burgeoning openness and desire for mental health support has burdened and stretched many practitioners in our field.

Counselors and life coaches who keep traditional hours find their schedules jampacked with back-to-back appointments. Practitioners who meet virtually with their clients day in and day out suffer from "Zoom fatigue." In many spaces, the demand for services outpaces the availability of qualified therapists.

For some, this pace of mental health care practice is unsustainable. Without some kind of change, you and your colleagues are going to burn out.

Maybe that's not your story. Maybe you aren't worried about burnout. Instead, you've noticed shortcomings in the traditional model of care. Meeting in one-hour sessions once a week, biweekly, or monthly works for clients with minor concerns, but others? There just doesn't seem like there's ever enough time or space to truly dig in and address your clients' root issues. Just as you've begun to get somewhere, the clock ticks to the end of the hour, leaving you and your client with a huge gap until you can press in again.

And who knows if you'll be able to jump right back in with the same degree of attention and clarity next time.

The truth is there are some issues in our lives that can't be solved in hour-long sessions spread out over weeks, months, or even years.

What if you were able to spend longer increments of time with just one client? What if you could focus all of your energy and resources on helping just one couple, or a small group of people with similar challenges, over the course of days instead of hours?

Your practice—and your clients' lives—would be transformed.

The Intensive Method

I'm thrilled to introduce you to this powerful model of intensive therapy and its transformative potential for your clinical practice.

Intensives provide a framework for clinical practice that empowers clinicians to offer another way for their clients to meet their treatment goals.

At their core, 3-day intensives are concentrated therapeutic sessions spanning three consecutive days. Their goal is to achieve in-depth exploration and resolution within a short timeframe.

For the right kinds of clients, intensive therapy can offer:

- Quicker, efficient results and a more immediate impact on a client's mental health
- Crisis intervention to provide timely, focused support during a critical situation
- Focused therapeutic goals a client can work on during this concentrated time
- Experiential and immersive therapeutic techniques to enhance the therapeutic process
- Convenience for those whose schedules prohibit them from committing to regular, weekly sessions or for those who have to travel from a long distance
- Time-sensitive attention for clients who are preparing for major life decisions
- Intensive learning that allows clients to immerse themselves in therapeutic work

But perhaps most of all, intensives offer your clients **hope**. Numerous studies suggest that clients who participate in intensive therapy not only experience faster symptom relief, but also report feeling more hopeful, empowered, and confident in themselves—often for the first time in years.[1] This puts them on a track for greater healing and wellness as they continue their journey.

The Intensive Method can be used to deliver many different therapeutic treatments, for many different conditions clients face. It is a flexible and accommodating method of delivery that both counselors and life coaches can shape to meet their individual specialties and preferences as well as the particular needs of their clients. That's part of the power of this delivery method—it delivers a customized therapeutic experience unlike anything you'd be able to accomplish within the traditional delivery method.

Let's take a look at more of the differences between traditional therapy and The Intensive Method.

Traditional Therapy vs. The Intensive Method - Timeframe of Treatment

One of the most obvious benefits of The Intensive Method is the timeframe of treatment—intensive therapy aims to achieve significant progress in a short period of time.

The standard intensive length we'll reference throughout this manual is three days, but you can also use this model to deliver concentrated intensives that are two days, one day, or half days that can stand alone or be added onto other intensive sessions.

Traditional Therapy vs. The Intensive Method - Depth and Intensity of Exploration

There are some clients who benefit more from the traditional therapeutic method, which allows them to gradually explore their concerns over a longer period of time.

---

1 *Intensive Prolonged Exposure and EMDR for PTSD: A Pilot Study* (van Woudenberg et al., 2018); *Narrative Exposure Therapy for survivors of multiple and complex trauma* (Schauer, Neuner, & Elbert, 2011); *Self-concept changes during intensive outpatient treatment for PTSD* (Held et al., 2021).

But other clients may be better suited for The Intensive Method's approach, which allows for a deeper exploration of their patterns, behaviors, and psycho-education in a concentrated amount of time.

Traditional Therapy vs. The Intensive Method - Immersion and Focus

There are some clients who need the time and space that traditional therapy affords them to process and integrate the insights they discover through your sessions.

The immersive experience of an intensive, however, gives clients a much more concentrated experience, which can promote rapid growth. It's kind of like a summer camp experience—any time you remove yourself from your everyday environment and enter a structured and programmed environment designed to achieve specific goals, rapid growth is bound to take place.

This rapid growth will likely need to be sustained in some kind of ongoing aftercare, group therapy, 12-step program, or traditional therapy, which we'll get into later.

Traditional Therapy vs. The Intensive Method - Client Commitment

Both kinds of therapy require commitments from your client in order for them to experience the rewards of their experience—traditional therapy requires an ongoing commitment over an extended period of time, while The Intensive Method demands a significant commitment upfront for a much shorter period of time.

Traditional Therapy vs. The Intensive Method - Crisis and Stabilization

Traditional delivery methods of care and The Intensive Method do not have to be an either-or option; in fact, The Intensive Method is a great option to help your clients address acute issues or crisis situations, establish a solid foundation for recovery, and then move on to traditional therapy or other support services.

The two forms of therapy can go hand-in-hand.

Traditional Therapy vs. The Intensive Method - Therapeutic Techniques

It's of course possible to integrate a variety of therapeutic modalities into a traditional approach to therapy, but in an intensive setting, you have greater freedom and flexibility to use specific techniques, like Eye-Movement Desensitization and Reprocessing (EMDR), Internal Family Systems, Somatic Experiencing Therapy, Acceptance and Commitment Therapy, and Solution Focused Brief Therapy.

It's also an excellent setting to really customize the therapeutic experience for your client.

Traditional Therapy vs. The Intensive Method - Logistical Considerations

There are straightforward and established expectations of service when it comes to traditional mental health sessions—your clients schedule an appointment, go through the intake process, attend a regular timeslot in your calendar, and schedule follow-up appointments according to your mutual availability. That's it.

On the other hand, intensives require a lot of logistical planning to be successful. Often, your clients will need to travel, set aside time from their work schedules, arrange for housing and meals, find childcare, and more, all to make space for an intensive.

You'll need to do a lot more logistical planning to offer intensives than your traditional services, but of course that's why you're here! We'll get into all of the logistics that will help you establish a strong and successful intensive plan throughout this book.

Traditional Therapy vs. The Intensive Method - Impact and Change

This is probably one of the most exciting aspects of offering intensives as a mental health practitioner.

Intensives aim to deliver immediate and impactful change. The people who come to an intensive typically leave the intensive forever changed for the better in just a few short days. It's exciting and powerful to witness and help people make these dramatic life changes.

You can facilitate that kind of change over the course of time in traditional therapy too, but it's more gradual. For the right clients, an intensive can accelerate substantial change.

Why Now? The Shifting Landscape of Mental Health Care

At the beginning of this chapter, I outlined why making this shift is a good idea, but it's more than that: it's a strategic and client-centered move that will revolutionize the way you practice.

Intensives are:

- Efficient
- Effective
- Client-centered
- Clinician-sustaining
- Grounded in emerging research and evidence-based methods

Statistically, more and more adults across the country are seeking out help from mental health professionals. According to the NIH, from 1999 to 2018, the percentage of the U.S. adult population who utilized mental health care increased from 7% to 11.3%.[2] And according to the CDC in 2020 this percentage increased to 20.8% across all ages and races for all mental health care, which also includes those taking medications for mental health conditions.[3]

As the stigma surrounding mental health challenges continues to erode, more and more Americans who suffer from various conditions will seek out various therapeutic methods to help them recover and heal. Among the rising demands for mental health care, intensives can potentially allow you to serve more clients in less time, bypassing traditional models by offering rapid, focused support for clients in crisis or transition.

Our clients are more aware and educated about specialized help, and they are actively seeking practitioners who offer it. When you promote that you offer intensives, you position yourself as a leader and a specialist, someone who

---

2 https://www.ncbi.nlm.nih.gov/pmc/articles/PMC10496400/

3 https://www.cdc.gov/nchs/data/databriefs/db419.pdf

provides intentional care that stands out from traditional practices.

When a client feels bogged down by the slow progress they experience in traditional settings, the concentrated approach of an intensive can accelerate breakthroughs, prevent drop-off, and provide a sense of momentum and empowerment.

High-functioning adults, busy professionals, trauma survivors, and more are hungry for a more tailored therapy experience. Intensives deliver a custom-designed experience that allows practitioners to incorporate multiple modalities into a seamless experience, one that offers depth and flexibility all at once.

Speaking of modalities, therapeutic treatments that are trauma-informed, somatic, and experiential—such as EMDR, IFS, ART, and SE—are becoming more mainstream and evidence-based, and these approaches are prime for the intensive model. In an intensive, there's time and space to regulate, reprocess, and reintegrate without being rushed out of the door after 50 minutes.

And let us not forget that **clinician burnout is a real crisis**. Therapists and coaches have to seek smarter ways to work with fewer clients and more impact. Intensives deliver fewer clients, fewer transitions, and more meaningful work. You can earn more while doing less, without sacrificing clinical excellence.

Now is the time to take up the call to practice mental health differently in our communities. You can make this happen.

CHAPTER 2

The Promise of Intensives

Much like you, I felt called to be a counselor. It gives me a deep sense of satisfaction to be able to help someone else find healing and wholeness in their lives. But feeling called to your profession does not make you immune to burnout. Helping people day in and day out can lead to empathy fatigue and exhaustion.

As the stigma surrounding mental health continues to dissolve, more and more people are seeking the help of clinicians. We need to be free and equipped to effectively handle the demand for our services, without putting ourselves and our families through unnecessary suffering.

Transitioning to intensive therapy provides a compelling pathway forward, to make your practice sustainable and to deliver results for your clients.

Client Breakthroughs, Clinician Fulfillment

As I mentioned in the previous chapter, the condensed structure of an intensive gives you far greater scheduling flexibility than the traditional weekly therapeutic rhythm. The optimized intensive schedule makes space for better work-life balance. You still need to implement and maintain appropriate boundaries for yourself, but the model itself makes those boundaries easier to enforce.

Wouldn't it be amazing to be able to spend hours and hours in the area you're most fascinated by in your field of study? Intensives are a perfect setting for exploring and expanding your professional capacity in that area. Intensives give you the time and space needed to deepen your area of expertise, exponentially increasing your specialty-based hours of practice. At the same time, intensives give you greater flexibility and freedom to experiment with a variety of therapeutic formats and techniques. The space for professional growth can reignite your passion for counseling while bringing fresh energy and joy to your practice.

Ultimately, the most important factor you need to consider when transitioning to intensives is how it will impact your clients. Intensive therapy is not for everyone—it isn't perfect for every client, and it isn't perfect for every clinician. Personally, I've found that the immersive nature of intensive therapy fosters a deeper connection between me and my clients. And for those clients who are committed and serious about doing the hard work that an intensive takes, I've seen significantly higher client satisfaction and more positive outcomes than what may have been possible in a traditional therapeutic setting.

More Revenue, More Time

You are probably wondering how it is that you could spend less time with fewer clients and make more money. The formula doesn't seem to compute, does it? Here's the deal: ***the specialization and concentrated amount of time required for intensives comes at a higher price tag for clients, which means an increase in revenue for your business.*** Each intensive gives you a guaranteed 15-20 hours of pay for three days worked.

The personalized attention you are able to dedicate to one individual's situation (or one couple's, or a small group of people) plus the expertise you bring with you into that setting *is worth their money.* I promise. If you're doubting yourself in this area, I have a whole section later on in this book about dealing with imposter syndrome—we'll get there, just stick with me. For now you need to keep reminding yourself: If you have invested in the training and you know what you're doing, you can deliver effective, profitable intensives. Believe it.

There are other reasons why intensives can generate increased revenue for your business. For one thing, other practitioners in your region are less likely to be offering specialized intensives like yours, providing you with more market differentiation. Intensives also appeal to a different, broader range of clients with varying needs and preferences than individuals who request traditional sessions.

The Right Kind of Client... and Clinician

As appealing as intensives seem from a profit margin standpoint, intensive therapy is not for everyone. It requires a significant commitment from clients who must be highly motivated to put in the hard work that intensive therapy demands.

And intensive therapy isn't for every clinician either! Clinicians who lead intensives have to put in extensive time and energy to plan and customize the client's experience. An intensive does more than deliver therapeutic services; you are crafting a therapeutic experience that requires a high degree of intentionality and structure.

If that sounds like a challenge you're willing to take on, then keep reading!

Assessing the Demand for Intensives in Your Community

Even if you feel like you are capable and qualified to lead intensives, there are other factors that you should consider before launching into this delivery method. You wouldn't be reading this if you didn't already think there's a need and demand for intensives...but is there, *really?* Market research can help you determine how receptive the community you serve will be to a new method of therapeutic service. You can start small and conduct some research with your own clients. Simply survey them to find out what areas of work they would like to do a deeper dive in, gain more psychoeducation, or accelerate their growth and healing.[4]

You should also ask yourself whether The Intensive Method makes sense for your area of specialization. Does it suit the demographics in your region of the country? When you look around your community, what gaps or emerging needs do you see, and how can you fill them? Is there space for this kind of therapy in your community?

---

4 *A market research survey template is available in The Intensive Method online course or as part of The Intensive Method Companion Workbook. Visit theintensivemethod.com to learn more.*

Thanks to the broad adaptation of telehealth services and the wealth of resources available out there to supplement your services, it's easier than ever to support client care all across the United States. Intensives open up your practice to people all over America without violating any state regulations. Still, it's important to evaluate the needs and demands in your own backyard. It will be easier for you to build a strong network locally, first, than to try to reach a national audience right away.

Regardless, now is the time to be asking these questions before you get too far into this adventure.

What many people fail to see when promoting their counseling or coaching business is that "the riches are in the niches." It's tempting for therapists and life coaches to market themselves as generalists, fearing that if they focus too much on a specialty niche, they will miss out on other clients they might be able to serve.

You need to resist this temptation, especially with intensives.

When considering investing in new specializations and certifications, it's important to think about several key factors: What will this cost me, and how well will it bring a return on my investment. For example, most clients search out therapists based on problems they face, not modalities we offer. So how can you define your speciality to include the problems you are an expert in solving, rather than just a modality you have paid a great deal for that clients don't even know what the initials mean?

If you have a passion about trauma or addiction, wouldn't it be great if you could promote an intensive to treat trauma and addiction, and then have the credentials to back up your expertise in your bio, versus trying to promote general therapy sessions with a credential that a run-of-the-mill client wouldn't know how to define?

As you build out your practice, you want to foster a culture of learning to continuously improve the quality of your intensives. The times are always changing, new therapies and research are in development constantly, and you want your business to be as relevant and impactful as possible to meet the needs of your clients. Foster a culture of adaptability within your practice to respond proactively to changing client needs and market dynamics.

If you are a group practice owner, you need to stay connected with industry associations, attend conferences, and participate in forums to stay informed about the latest trends and research in intensives. There are plenty of professional groups and associations out there who are practicing using intensives. Find your tribe, and participate in the broader conversation!

It is important for you to not only be excellent at your craft, but to stand out above the rest. Certainly having field specialities will help, but imagine, not only will you stand out as a highly skilled clinician in the areas of your passion, you will now also provide a unique way of delivering it. Over the last decade, when I've met people and shared about my intensive-based therapy practice, it's almost always followed by a question of intrigue and/or interest. People want to know how they can learn more about offering intensives personally.

Know Your Neighborhood

Familiarize yourself with the other businesses in your community that might be able to enhance your practice. These tangential competitors could actually serve as partners to your intensive practice, enhancing your client's experience. Businesses such as wellness retreats and spas, hotels and resorts, holistic health centers, fitness and yoga studios, and even bookstores or coffee shops could be partners that could turn your client's intensive into a retreat experience.

While you're eyeing the community for business partnership opportunities, don't forget to keep tabs on what your competitors are up to as well, so that you are able to gauge your own services, quality of care, and fee structure against the marketplace.

If you haven't already, work to establish strong relationships with primary care physicians, psychiatrists, and other healthcare providers who may refer clients to your intensive services. Traditional therapists might even be one of your target audiences—perhaps you yourself have seen the way intensives have helped your traditional clients. There are likely dozens of local clinicians who aren't aware of this method that are also not that interested in offering intensives. These folks could make great partners for you down the road.

Additional partnerships with community organizations and schools are also great ways to generate potential referrals, depending on your target demographic. Consider how you could partner with your local lawyers, mediators, police and first responders. You might consider offering free workshops or informational sessions to introduce potential clients or other clinicians to the benefits of intensives. You can also sponsor or participate in local events to raise awareness about mental health and well-being to contribute to the local community and as a way to promote your services.

Think in terms of what you can offer that would enhance the work of other professionals without creating a spirit of competition, but rather collaboration. For example, if you love to practice EMDR, let other general therapists in your area know you offer a special 3-Day EMDR Intensive, available especially for their clients as an adjunctive experience to accelerate healing and provide greater support in a short time frame.

When you offer to collaborate with the referring clinician, you will build a referral network at the same time! Win-Win!

Scalability & Flexibility

Most likely, you're already running a traditional mental health practice or are a part of one. How much flexibility does your practice have to handle an increase in clients seeking intensives? Is your practice established in such a way as to allow for scalability? How much control do you have over your current schedule and client load? Do you prefer more clients—or perhaps more hours with less clients—and more revenue?

If you're trying to shift away from offering traditional services towards offering exclusively intensives, you may want to consider partnerships with other mental health professionals to share resources and expertise, develop referral partnerships, and be able to continue meeting the needs of existing clients.

However, it isn't necessary to completely shift. In fact, I used a hybrid model for almost a decade. Part of that time was as a solo practitioner and part of the time was as a group practice owner, where I could focus more on my intensive-based clients and my team could do more of the week-to-week maintenance therapy.

That's one of the beautiful things about this model—you can quite literally create a custom approach that fits your exact practice goals and needs.

All of this upfront research will help you clearly articulate the unique benefits and outcomes clients can expect from your intensive therapy services.

Define your services and your specializations, but keep it simple! You might have lots of ideas for a variety of different intensives you could offer, but start with one or two solid core offerings that you can practice, fine tune, and evaluate...before you try to roll out a lot of different variations.

In the coming pages, we will tackle everything you need to structure and plan out intensives for your practice confidently. But before we get into the nitty gritty details of planning intensives, it's important that we lay the groundwork for some basic ethical considerations and boundaries that may differ from your traditional therapeutic delivery methods.

CHAPTER 3

Ethical Considerations and Boundaries

When transitioning from traditional services to offering intensives, it's essential to understand that you're not just changing the length of the session—you're reimagining the entire therapeutic process. A 3-day intensive condenses months of therapeutic work into a highly focused, deeply immersive experience. This shift requires counselors and coaches to approach treatment differently—ethically, practically, and relationally.

In this chapter, we'll explore the critical ethical considerations that come with this model: from managing client expectations and setting firm boundaries, to maintaining confidentiality, fostering autonomy, and ensuring proper aftercare. These elements aren't just checkboxes—they're what allow you to offer a powerful, transformative experience with integrity and care. Whether you're just starting to imagine this model or already preparing to launch, this content will give you the foundation you need to practice ethically and effectively.

In traditional mental health care services, the time frame you work with a client is often extended, with sessions occurring regularly over weeks, months, or even years. The therapeutic relationship tends to develop gradually, as you and your client explore issues together over time.

Intensives, on the other hand, concentrate 4-6 months of traditional therapy into a much shorter timespan. The timespan typically lasts no more than three days, but in some cases up to five days or as few as one or two. This compressed schedule requires a much more focused and targeted approach.

You need to get in and get started quickly, tackling ethical considerations and establishing boundaries with your clients in ways that are different from what you're likely accustomed to.

Informed Consent and Client Expectations

In traditional therapy, informed consent is crucial, but the process may be more ongoing, allowing for adjustments and deeper exploration of issues as they arise over multiple sessions.

In intensive therapy, clients need clearly communicated goals, expectations, and potential outcomes from the outset. Transparent communication is crucial to ensure that clients understand the nature of the short-term commitment, allowing them to make informed decisions about their participation.

This is one reason you should consider offering a screening call, sales funnel (fancy term for sales page and process), and a webinar or a hybrid of those options. You want to be very clear from the onset what you are offering, the approach you will use, and specific goals you plan to achieve.

Therapeutic Relationship and Boundaries

Here are some tips for ethically managing your therapeutic relationships and establishing boundaries with your clients:

- **Establish Rapport Quickly:** Intensive therapy requires establishing and maintaining therapeutic rapport quickly.
- **Clarify Roles and Expectations:** Clearly define the roles of both the therapist and the client in the context of intensive therapy. Explicitly communicate your expectations regarding the therapeutic process, goals, and the client's role in achieving them.
- **Managing Transference and Countertransference:** Due to the condensed nature of intensive therapy, you should be attuned to potential transference and countertransference dynamics. Regular supervision and self-awareness are crucial to manage these dynamics ethically.
- **Setting Clear Boundaries:** Establish and communicate clear professional boundaries from the outset. It's crucial to avoid blurring the lines between therapeutic roles and personal relationships.

- **Addressing Resistance and Ambivalence:** In the short duration of intensive therapy, therapists may encounter resistance or ambivalence from clients. Paying attention to these dynamics and skillfully addressing them is crucial for making progress within the limited timeframe. We'll cover this more in later lessons.
- **Cultural Sensitivity:** Be attentive to the diverse cultural backgrounds of clients in intensive therapy. Therapists should be mindful of how cultural factors may impact the therapeutic relationship and tailor interventions accordingly.
- **Navigating Intense Emotions:** Given the intensity of the therapeutic work, therapists must skillfully navigate and manage intense emotions that may arise quickly. This includes providing a supportive space for clients to express themselves while ensuring emotional safety.
- **Regular Check-Ins:** Schedule regular check-ins within the intensive therapy period to assess the client's experience, address emerging issues, and ensure that the therapeutic process remains collaborative and attuned to the client's needs.
- **Termination and Closure:** Plan for termination and closure from the beginning of the intensive. Discussing and preparing for the end of your services helps manage expectations and provides a sense of closure for both the clinician and the client. However, keep in mind with intensives, clients often want to return for years... and that's okay. You don't have to terminate them. If you continue to work with them, you will take note of that in your session records. We'll go over continuing care in more detail later, but just make sure that you address this important topic at the onset.
- **Providing Psychoeducation:** Offer psychoeducation about the nature of intensives, including goals, limitations, and the expected intensity of the process. This empowers clients to actively engage in their therapeutic journey.
- **Flexibility in Approaches:** Be adaptable and flexible in therapeutic approaches. The condensed timeframe may require adjustments to traditional therapeutic techniques to meet the immediate needs of the client effectively.
- **Monitoring and Self-Care:** Given the intense nature of the work,

actively monitor your own well-being and don't forget to practice self-care. Regular supervision, debriefing, and reflective practices are crucial to maintain your own resilience.

Depth of Exploration and Scope of Practice

Intensives are typically focused on addressing immediate concerns and achieving specific goals. The limited amount of time you have with your clients in an intensive requires you to focus on issues that can be addressed effectively within the available time frame, avoiding the risk of overstepping professional boundaries or attempting interventions outside your competence.

Confidentiality and Privacy

Confidentiality remains a critical consideration in both short-term and traditional therapy. However, in short-term intensive therapy, therapists must find a balance between creating a safe space for participants to share and the limited time available.

It is important that you are able to establish boundaries regarding what information will be covered within the short time frame and how confidentiality will be maintained. Since you will only have a brief couple of days together with your client, participants may be more reluctant to share personal information without assurances of privacy. Clearly articulated guidelines on confidentiality foster a safe therapeutic environment and will help you establish trust early on in your intensives.

The pre-intensive onboarding process for clients is an integral part of establishing these boundaries and building trust before a client arrives for their intensive. We'll go into greater detail about these processes later.

Goal Setting and Achievability

There is a lot you can cover in three days... but also, there's only so much you can cover in three days! You will set up your clients for the best outcomes by establishing realistic and achievable goals for the intensive.

The work that you do leading up to the intensive to gather a client's history, emotions, and experiences will inform and shape a rich, dynamic intensive session for your client. Still, your content needs to remain focused on the objectives you've outlined in advance.

Participants need to have a clear understanding of what can be accomplished in the short duration. Unrealistic expectations may lead to disappointment and dissatisfaction with the therapy process.

Participant Autonomy

You are the guide and the one responsible for shaping the client experience during their intensive therapy, but that doesn't mean you will dictate every aspect of their experience. It's important to promote participant autonomy and involve your clients in decision-making, even and especially within the limited timeframe.

Your participants should feel empowered to actively engage in their therapeutic process. Respecting autonomy contributes to a more collaborative and ethical therapeutic relationship.

Emergency Procedures and Crisis Management

Although it's right there in the name, it can't be overstated: intensives are INTENSE! This deep and concentrated exploration of your clients' circumstances and background can put a lot of strain on their well-being in the off-hours of their therapy sessions with you.

Therapists need to have clear emergency procedures in place, and they need to communicate those emergency procedures to their clients clearly so they know how to access support outside of their scheduled therapy hours. The time-limited nature of intensive therapy requires a proactive approach to handle potential crises swiftly. Participants should be informed about available support in case of emergencies.

Follow-up and Aftercare

Although intensives take place in a short time span, intensive therapy isn't a one-and-done magic wand for mental health. It can accelerate a person's recovery, and it can provide a strong foundation for their healing, but your clients may also need information on available resources and aftercare options beyond the intensive.

Follow-up and aftercare is an essential ingredient to your client's ongoing recovery journey. It is your ethical responsibility to acknowledge the potential for ongoing challenges beyond the intensive and to facilitate connections to longer term therapy or support services if participants have ongoing therapeutic needs.

We will go into greater depth about aftercare in later chapters.

As you can see, offering intensives is not simply about doing more therapy in less time—it's about creating a thoughtfully structured, ethically sound, and client-centered experience from start to finish. So what does that client-centered experience look like, really? In our next chapter, we'll walk through the core components of an intensive, from what happens before a client even steps into the room to what unfolds during the experience, and then how to ensure meaningful support afterward. We'll also talk more about how you can tailor your intensives to suit your clinical specialty and your client population.

CHAPTER 4

The Anatomy of an Intensive

We've spent a good deal of time thinking about how intensives differ from traditional delivery methods, whether or not intensives are right for you and your clientele, and the differences between intensives and traditional mental health services regarding ethics and boundaries. But other than a more concentrated period of time, what does an intensive look like?

Let's walk through an overview of the mechanics of The Intensive Method, beginning with what needs to be done to prepare for an intensive, how a typical 3-day intensive is structured, and what aftercare and follow-up looks like on the other end of an intensive. This chapter will provide you with a mile-high view of intensives; in later chapters, we'll zoom in to help you build out the details of your particular intensive.

Planning and Preparation in 10 Steps

The success of your intensives depends upon the work you do in the weeks leading up to your client's arrival. These steps are critical for your client's success. Onboarding your clients is a back-and-forth process, with a role for both the client and the clinician each step of the way. We'll go over the client screening and assessment process in greater detail in Part 4. For now, imagine that you've already accepted your client for their intensive. We've identified ten steps to follow to ensure a smooth onboarding process for your client.

Step One: Client Completes Pre-Assessment Forms

Several weeks prior to the scheduled intensive, you will send your client a list of pre-assessment forms they need to complete, which will include history and background information that will help you understand your client's history and concerns. I recommend incorporating validated assessment tools and inventories to gather quantitative data that can help you measure your client's progress throughout the intensive. We'll dig into these specific forms and offer you some templates to help you with onboarding in a later chapter.

Step Two: Review Client Information

Once your client has completed this material, you'll want to thoroughly review the client's pre-assessment information, history, and any other relevant documentation to be well-informed prior to the intensive. This will contribute to the work in your next step.

Step Three: Clarify Goals and Expectations with the Client

As part of your pre-assessment communications, you will need to communicate the goals and expectations of the 3-day intensive to the client clearly to make sure there is mutual understanding about the therapeutic process.

But goal setting needs to be a collaborative process! Your client should share their own specific goals and objectives for the intensive to make sure that you are in alignment. The two of you together can identify key themes your client wants to address, which will help you focus your planning for the intensive.

In addition to their own goals, it's important for your client to understand and discuss with you the expectations, format, and structure of their intensive. You don't want there to be any gray area or confusion about what they're getting into—this is a big commitment for them and a substantial investment of time, resources, and emotional energy. Everyone needs to be on the same page.

Step Four: Prepare Your Therapeutic Materials

Based on the content and goals discussed with your client, you will then prepare your therapeutic materials, exercises, and interventions. This is where it gets fun! Intensives offer you so many opportunities to customize the therapeutic experience for your clients.

Step Five: Coordinate Logistics

Many clients travel from other areas of the region or even from other parts of the country for intensives, so your onboarding process needs to pay close attention to coordinating logistics. This involves logistics during your intensive, such as scheduling, breaks, and additional support they might need during the intensive, as well as helping them understand the logistics getting to and leaving your location.

In my practice, it is up to my clients to make travel plans and accommodations (if necessary) for their intensives. We have an onsite suite that clients can use if they'd like, but we also point them in the direction of area hotels and restaurants if they prefer to stay offsite. Some simple reminders about childcare, petcare, packing lists, and so on can help them feel less anxious about the process. You might also offer your clients some additional services that can ensure a comfortable and focused experience, such as wrap-around retreat activities, tourist opportunities, natural attractions in the area, and so on.

Step Six: Create a Comfortable Environment

Your clients are going to be spending a lot of time with you in your setting. If you are holding your intensives in an office setting, arrange it in such a way as to be comfortable and conducive for therapy. If you will be in a different location, make sure that your space for therapy provides privacy as well as space for your client to relax.

Step Seven: Guide Your Client to Prepare Emotionally for the Intensive

While you're preparing the material for the intensive, your client needs to make space to prepare emotionally and mentally for the intensive experience. You can remind them that this session will probably be an emotionally challenging time and may require openness to explore deep-seated issues. Alerting them to this will help them prepare, but you can also offer them some tools to mentally prepare for their experience.

Either prior to a client's arrival or immediately upon arrival, your client should develop a self-care plan for the duration of the intensive. This should include practices or activities that promote well-being and emotional balance.

Step Eight: Prepare Yourself for Emotional Intensity

It's no small task for the clinician to spend three days with a client, either! It's important that you take care of your own well-being leading up to an intensive so that you are in the right headspace to help others in their headspace. You can do this through engaging in self-reflection practices, seeking supervision and consultation with other colleagues, maintaining your own therapeutic support through ongoing personal therapy, practicing mindfulness and grounding techniques, or developing some pre-session rituals to give yourself time and space to become calm and focused.

Step Nine: Establish Emergency Protocols

Discuss and establish emergency protocols with your client, including contact information for crisis support or additional resources if needed.

Step Ten: Complete Necessary Intake Forms

Before the intensive begins, your client needs to sign consent forms, release of information forms, and any other required documentation. Typically, we have our clients complete this information on the day they arrive. And of course, you need to ensure that all necessary documentation, consent forms, and legal requirements are in place and compliant with ethical and legal standards.

Don't forget, open communication during the preparation phase of an intensive is critical to laying the foundation for a collaborative and supportive environment. Following these steps ensures your intensive will be beneficial and effective for your client.

3-Day Intensive Structure: Past, Present, Future

Your client has been emailing you regularly, submitting their forms, getting excited and nervous at the same time, and now, the day is finally here! Your client is ready and waiting for you in your lobby. What will the next three days look like?

While you can design your intensive within any time frame ranging from a half-day to five days, I've found that three days is a sweet spot for the kind of work most of us hope to accomplish with our clients in an intensive setting.

For that reason, I think about the intensive experience in three parts, divided simply enough over three days:

Day 1 is all about the **past**.

Day 2 focuses on the **present**.

And Day 3 turns your client's attention to the **future**.

This structure is extremely intentional, designed to guide your client along a journey through their history, into the behaviors and conditions they are presently experiencing, and towards a vision of what their life can be like moving forward.

Let's take a closer look at each of these experiences.

3-Day Intensive, Day One

Taking what you've gathered during your pre-intensive onboarding process, you and your client will spend the majority of your time on Day 1 building rapport, reviewing the assessment results you've collected, going over your client's history and treatment goals, setting short- and long-term goals, and outlining the intensive focus areas.

Depending on the primary focus of care for your client, the topics and exercises may vary. However, keep in mind, Day 1 is all about helping you gather more information about your client, giving your client an opportunity to share their history, deepening the understanding of their presenting problems, and identifying patterns.

One of my favorite ways to foster these goals is utilizing a "Life Events Timeline" exercise. As part of the onboarding experience, I ask my client to prepare a timeline of their life events. I provide both an instructional sheet as well as a spreadsheet they can compile ahead of time. They may include significant events, people, and milestones in their life that have shaped and impacted them. These might include negative traumatic experiences as well as detailed positive experiences. An exercise like this may be used for any type of therapy and for any sort of therapeutic goals you may have for your ideal client.[5]

Starting and/or ending each session with an emotional check-in is another tried and true Intensive Method exercise. I personally use a flip chart of emotions, beginning in the first session of Day 1. By Day 3, my clients know they will be doing a "feelings check" to start every session of each day together.

In addition to this feelings check, you might consider ending each day with a review, asking your client to consider, take notes, and share some of the defining moments of the day. This will help them have a collection of defining moments that contributed to creating a powerful experience by the end of the intensive, and it will also serve as a reminder when they reflect on their intensive in the days ahead.

---

5 *The Life Events Timeline exercise instructions and spreadsheet are available as part of The Intensive Method Companion Workbook or as a download through The Intensive Method website. Visit theintensivemethod.com to learn more.*

3-Day Intensive, Day Two

Having spent a lot of time in a client's past on Day 1, Day 2 will focus on the present.

To be clear, this doesn't mean we are drawing a line in the past and saying there's no need to discuss it further. Make sure you are clear with your client that this is not what you mean, nor would that be healthy. As long as they have wounds from the past, they need to be able to discuss and process the past.

Rather, the focus on Day 2 regarding the present is how the past is impacting the present, taking time to carefully consider how the past has and is shaping, influencing, and impacting your client in their present set of circumstances.

Process and exercises on Day 2 should be focused on identifying these critical factors and giving your client practical ways to address their present mindstate and the areas of concern that require treatment.

There are many ways you will go about doing this. Creating your own portfolio of exercises and interventions will come with time. However, here are a few things to consider: find ways to turn toward targeted therapeutic interventions, immersive work to address specific issues, skill building practice, self-reflection encouragement, and ways to deepen introspection and self-exploration.

You are an excellent, skilled, qualified clinician, and my suggestion is to gather the tools in your toolbelt you currently offer in traditional spaces, but consider systematizing them in a way that you could pull from several over the course of Day 2.

One of my favorite exercises on Day 2 is to go back through the timeline from Day 1 and specifically highlight entries that were especially impactful. Then, take each one of those and unpack them, deepening the insights around feelings and emotions, cognitions, and preferred outcomes. This could be done for trauma work as well, honing in on negative emotions and cognitions specifically.

You will have covered a lot of ground with your client by the end of Day 2, which is a prime time to review their progress with them.

3-Day Intensive, Day Three

It's Day 3 already! And trust me, that is exactly how your clients will feel.

In almost all of my intensives, clients are amazed at how quickly the time goes.

On the final day together, your focus with your client is preparing them for life back in the "real world." Building upon the exercises you worked through the day before, you will continue targeted therapeutic work, discuss strategies for maintaining progress, develop a plan for ongoing support and follow-up, and summarize key insights and achievements.

It's a good exercise to have some form of a treatment plan that you compile with your client on Day 3. This may include some sort of summary but should be focused on the future. It should be specific, laying out a framework of goals and deliverables for your client.[6]

3-Day Intensive Structure and Rhythm

As you assemble your schedule for all three days of the intensive, keep in mind these tips:

Schedule Regular Check-Ins: We've discussed starting sessions with a Feelings Check, but if you prefer an alternate approach, schedule regular check-ins throughout the three days to gauge their emotional state and well-being. Find a consistent approach to do this and your client will experience the value because of your intention. It's a great opportunity to encourage them to do this on their own in the future, noting the benefits of self-reflection.

Take Breaks: Integrate short stretch breaks and encourage self-care to prevent emotional fatigue, both for your client and for yourself.

Be Flexible: Maintain flexibility to adapt to your client's needs and progress.

I'm excited to get through the structural content of these intensives and dive into the many and varied ways you can integrate experiential and immersive therapeutic techniques into your intensives. For now, let's turn to the last but certainly not least important part of the intensive: aftercare and follow-up.

---

6 *A sample treatment plan is included as part of The Intensive Method online course and is available for download at theintensivemethod.com.*

Aftercare and Follow-Up

Similar to the onboarding experience, the client and the clinician both have roles and expectations following an intensive experience. A quality aftercare program will help ensure ongoing client success as well as support your client's impression of the intensive experience itself. Here's another set of steps I recommend following to transition your client from the intensive to their regular life and onward into follow-up recovery:

Step One: Client and Clinician Develop an Aftercare Plan

As part of the third day's itinerary, I often work with my clients to develop their aftercare plan, but this can also be completed during a post-intensive review session. Collaborate with your client to establish a comprehensive aftercare plan, providing them guidance on self-care, coping strategies, and any ongoing support they might need to continue the therapeutic work.

If you've incorporated your client's prepared Life Events Timeline into the intensive, aftercare is an excellent opportunity to continue the work that manifested from that exercise. During the intensive, you might have a running task-list entitled, "Future Work for Aftercare." As you progress through sessions, you might cite specific topics for future work or "unfinished business" that you and your client acknowledge will need to be addressed at some point later, but not right now. Some examples of this could be empty chair work for resentments or amends, experiential exercises like EMDR or Brainspotting, or perhaps events they would like to expand upon down the road. The items identified on the "Future Work for Aftercare" list make a perfect and natural segue into discussing the next steps for your client's recovery plan.

Step Two: Schedule a Post-Intensive Review Session for Your Client

Beyond the intensive, you will want your client to schedule a follow-up session shortly after the intensive to review the experience, discuss insights gained, and address any immediate concerns or questions. This gives your client some time and distance to process the experience they had and its impact on their well-being.

This could be accomplished in several ways: You could have a feedback form, a phone call, or a Zoom consultation specifically for post-intensive review. Remember, you are tailoring your intensive experience, so it could be a variety of options depending on the client or the case sensitivity or complexity.

Step Three: Create a Post-Intensive Assessment

Following the review session, you will want to create a post-intensive assessment to evaluate the client's progress, determine the effectiveness of the intensive, and identify any ongoing therapeutic needs. Personally, I just add these notes at the bottom of my intensive session record under the heading "Considerations for Future Aftercare." Certainly if you would like to create a more formal assessment and tracking you may, and if you utilize practice software for your notes, this could be a good place to create a general note template for post-intensive notes, feedback and considerations.

Keep in mind, this is a great way to gain overall feedback from your clients and their intensive experience. Some of the feedback you gain will be specific to your client, and other feedback will be beneficial to you for your overall intensive strategy. Having a place for evaluations and general feedback will be very helpful as well.

On any assessment, feedback and/or evaluation forms, you can put a disclaimer that states we may use any positive feedback for testimonial purposes in the future, which would of course protect any personal information. These positive testimonials will be gems for you. Personally they will be inspiring and motivating, while also potentially serving as future marketing material.

Step Four: Client's Integration of Insights

Clients are expected to reflect on and integrate the insights they've gained during the intensive into their daily life, which includes applying their newly acquired coping skills and self-awareness as they navigate everyday challenges.

Step Five: Schedule Follow-Up Sessions with Your Client

If appropriate for your practice, you may want to schedule follow-up therapy sessions with your client or refer them to a traditional therapist (if they aren't already working with one) to address any emerging issues and support their ongoing growth.

Step Six: Ongoing Support for Your Client

Your client needs to understand that the intensive experience is not a magic wand that automatically fixes their lives. Intensives are intentionally outside of the client's regular routine. Obviously, if you've recommended ongoing therapy sessions, your client ought to engage in those sessions on a regularly scheduled basis to ensure continued progress along their healing journey.

Following their experience, if you recommend additional support services, such as group therapy, support groups, or other specialized resources that are aligned with your client's needs, you will need to coordinate those referrals.

Don't worry, we will discuss specifics with client care collaboration, obtaining proper releases, and coordination of client care as we continue; however, it is important to note, you should champion whatever adjunctive care you recommend for your clients and do what you can to ensure continuity of care.

Two important considerations:

First, make sure you have the proper releases signed at the initial intensive for any other collaborative clinicians and explain to your client your desire to work with them as a team to support their overall treatment goals. You can also explain they will need to provide a release for those clinicians.

Secondly, and this is very important: be sure to let clients know upfront that it is not your desire to replace other clinicians they are working with, and while it's always the client's decision, ultimately, how they choose treatment, you let them know upfront that this is a professional boundary for you.

Referrals from other clinicians will be very beneficial for you, and if other clinicians suspect you might be poaching their clients, they will be less inclined to refer to you. Having something stated in writing can certainly help clarify your intentions with clients and clinicians.

Typically, I connect with referring clinicians prior to the initial intensive to outline goals and boundaries, and for clinicians that are shared with me at the intensive, I connect with them immediately following the intensive. That point of contact may be a phone call or an email, or in some cases may be deferred, if the client prefers confidentiality or an opportunity to discuss with the outside clinician first.

In any case, be sure to address this important issue and solidify your preferred method of contact.[7]

---

7 *Post-intensive clinician follow-up, clinical templates, and other pre-intensive paperwork is included as part of The Intensive Method online course and is available for download from theintensivemethod.com.*

Step Seven: Monitor Your Client's Progress and Be Available for Support

Immediately following the intensive, make yourself available for any questions, concerns, or crises that may arise—this is a vulnerable time for most clients, and they might need the person who just helped them navigate some rough waters. Provide your clients with your contact information for emergencies.

Even if you are not your client's traditional therapist, you will want to monitor your client's progress with some degree of regularity, checking in with them every once in a while to adjust their treatment goals and interventions as needed, based on the post-intensive assessment. This is also an opportunity for you to invite them back for any additional intensive work that they might benefit from.

Your clients might need encouragement to maintain a line of open communication with you, so encourage them to report any significant changes, challenges, or successes they experience after the intensive.

Step Eight: Recommend Self-Care Practices

Encourage your client as part of their aftercare plan to prioritize self-care practices and activities that promote their emotional well-being, such as mindfulness, relaxation techniques, and other strategies they learned during the intensive.

Step Nine: Feedback, Iteration, and Follow-Up Assessments

In addition to the post-intensive assessment of your client, you should also invite your client to give you feedback on the intensive experience. This open communication can help you make adjustments and improvements to your therapeutic approaches.

Beyond the initial post-intensive assessments, you may want to issue follow-up assessments or evaluations to track your client's progress and adjust their treatment plan as needed. I have several assessments I give to my clients every time I see them. They complete a full battery of intake assessments prior to the initial intensive. From that list, I have a select few they take again on the morning of the first day of their 3-day intensive and again at every aftercare session.

These are scored and charted in my session notes in a graph format so I can track my client's progress over the course of treatment. Some general assessments I utilize are for depression, anxiety, and post-traumatic stress, to name a few. These should be personalized for your clientele should you choose to do something similar.

Step Ten: Documentation and Reporting

As intimately as you get to know your clients in these intensive experiences, we all need to maintain thorough documentation and reporting for every client. Document and report progress, changes, or challenges you observe during the post-intensive follow-up, and maintain accurate records to inform their ongoing treatment planning.

As you've seen in this chapter, delivering a high-impact 3-day intensive requires far more than simply blocking out time on your calendar. From thoughtful planning and emotional preparation to structured therapeutic rhythm and comprehensive aftercare, each phase of the intensive experience is carefully designed to support transformation. Now you have a mile-high view of how The Intensive Method works—how to set the stage, guide the process, and follow through with purpose and care.

But before you're able to build a clinically powerful intensive, you need to know who your intensives are for and how to reach them. You can't really design an intensive without knowing something about the people you hope to help. Our goal is to provide you with the direction and clarity to identify that audience and then build an intensive to meet that audience's needs.

In Part 2, we'll shift from the clinical to the strategic, guiding you through how to identify your ideal client, carve out your niche, and develop the marketing systems that will attract and convert the right people to your intensives. You'll learn how to build referral relationships, write compelling sales materials, and establish a brand identity that authentically reflects your values and specialization. We'll also explore how to package, price, and scale your intensives to meet your financial goals—all while keeping your clients' needs and outcomes at the center.

Ready to bring your intensive to the people who need it most?

PART 2

Building and Marketing Your Intensive

CHAPTER 5

Your Ideal Client & How to Reach Them

Have you ever stood in a crowded room and tried to get everyone's attention all at once? You raise your voice, wave your arms, maybe even stand on a chair. A few people glance your way, but most keep talking, distracted or uninterested. It takes an incredible amount of energy to grab *everyone's* attention. But what if you walked into that same room, locked eyes with one person, and spoke directly to their greatest need?

They'd lean in. They'd listen. They'd respond.

That's the power of narrowing your focus.

In a sea of voices, clarity is magnetic. Day and night, everyone and everything is demanding our undivided attention. How are you going to rise above the ruckus? As a coach or clinician offering intensives, your work is deep, personal, and often life-changing. But if your message is trying to appeal to everyone, it ends up resonating with no one. You don't need more noise; you need precision.

This chapter is about finding that precision, not just for marketing purposes, but to ensure that the work you're doing actually reaches the people who need it most. When you know your ideal client, everything becomes easier: how you design your intensive, how you speak about it, where you show up online, and how confident you feel charging what your work is worth. That's why we're turning to this subject now and not *after* you've crafted your intensive.

Let's start by exploring your niche, or the specific area of transformation you're equipped to offer. From there, you'll craft your client avatar, a detailed profile that helps you connect with the people you're best positioned to serve.

Because when you focus your message, you amplify your impact.

Identifying Your Niche and Crafting Your Avatar

I have designed several different intensives to address very specific goals in my practice. Those intensives have a set treatment plan template I use as my basis for planning, adapting as needed to accommodate my client's various needs. When I first began, I started with just one primary intensive, targeted to couples who were entering betrayal recovery together. Since then, I have expanded to offer many other types of intensive templates. If you're just starting out with intensives, you probably feel like you could develop several different intensives to meet a variety of needs. Or you might be inclined to develop a more generic intensive that could be adapted to your many specialties.

I urge you to resist that temptation. Intensives have enough moving pieces as it is, so before you start brainstorming many different variations and custom-tailored options, I recommend following the Build, Measure, Learn principle. Start with a Minimum Viable Product (or MVP), a simple, functional version of your idea. Then test out your intensive a couple of times, collecting data and feedback along the way. Finally, use what you've learned from those first few intensives to modify, refine, improve, or pivot. Once you're feeling good about your MVP, you can begin to explore how you can meet the needs of other niches and target audiences.

You're probably already chewing on ideas for your own intensive, but before you go any further, let's take a look at my friend Sheryl's brainstorming process.

From General to Specific: Sheryl's Story

Sheryl is a licensed counselor with a heart for helping people through grief. For years, she has offered traditional weekly sessions and is known in her community as someone you can turn to when life falls apart. When she began exploring intensives, her first instinct was to offer "Grief Intensives"—a space for anyone navigating loss to process their pain more deeply over a 2- or 3-day period.

However, the experience of grief is vast and varied. A 17-year-old grieving a parent's death needs something very different from a 72-year-old who just lost her spouse after 50 years. A man grieving a divorce doesn't always resonate with the same approach as a young mother mourning a miscarriage.

Sheryl cares about all these people, but trying to appeal to them all within the structural confines of one intensive felt overwhelming and confusing. Instead, I encouraged Sheryl to look back at the clients who had made the most profound breakthroughs during her care—and who had left her feeling deeply fulfilled as a clinician. One group stood out: recently widowed individuals.

That was her *sweet* spot. She understood their silence, their shock, and their fear of the empty bed. She knew the unique emotional weight of losing a life partner, and she had developed tools, metaphors, and rituals that spoke directly into that space. So she narrowed her niche.

When Sheryl makes this shift, instead of offering general grief intensives, she will focus her intensive on a more specific topic, gearing her 3-day intensive to the newly widowed.

This small shift can change everything. Sheryl's messaging becomes sharper. Her ideal client feels clearly seen. Referral partners know exactly who to send her way. And best of all—**Sheryl feels more energized and effective** because she is showing up in the space where she could do her best work.

What's Your Niche?

So, what's your niche? Think about your areas of expertise and your areas of passion. Think back on your years of serving clients. What scenarios felt the most fulfilling to you as a coach or clinician? How can you get more specific about your area of expertise?

Matching Your Target Audience to Your Niche

By now, you likely have in mind the primary focus of your intensive. Thinking through your niche goes hand-in-hand with defining your target audience. Like Sheryl's story above, you probably can picture the type of person who will most benefit from this intensive.

In order to create the avatar for your target audience, you're going to need to engage in a little bit of stereotyping. Obviously, every single person is unique and will bring their distinct personalities to your therapy practice, but there are some things your clients will likely hold in common. Your target audience will help you focus on who it is you want to reach, understanding that there will be some folks who land farther outside that target as well as those who completely hit the bullseye.

Defining your target audience will help you develop the appropriate messaging and tactics later on to attract the right customers in the right places. This isn't meant to exclude anyone, but rather to help you zero in and focus on who the right person is that needs the intensives that you offer.

We recommend identifying two to three different personas, beginning with the most likely to use your service and moving outward from there.

Let's return to the example of Sheryl's grief intensive. When Sheryl thought about her current clientele, the majority of her sessions tended to be with newly widowed women in their 70s and up. This group tends to face unique challenges, like social isolation, shifting identities after decades of marriage, and long-term caregiving fatigue. They're also a high potential audience, because they often have more time and motivation to engage deeply in healing work.

This is the target audience and avatar Sheryl should design her intensive around. The same intensive could also meet the needs of recently widowed men, usually between the ages of 65-80.

Sometimes, the person shopping for help isn't the person who needs the help, so as Sheryl thinks about promoting her intensive, she might also keep in mind the adult children of the recently widowed. They may recognize the signs that their parent needs help recovering from their loss, and they may be the one who goes hunting for help online.

Now, Sheryl has three different target audiences in mind for her grief intensive. Who is your primary target audience, the group or type of person who is most often seeking support in your area of expertise? Stay with your target audience for a little while, answering the following questions about them:

- How old are they?
- What gender are they?
- What stage of life are they in?
- What common challenges are they facing related to your service?
- What do they stand to gain from participating in your service?

As you define your various avatars for your intensive, you will use these personas to tailor your marketing messages to resonate with the specific concerns and aspirations of your target demographic.

Once you've identified your niche and crafted a clear picture of your ideal client, the next step is to connect with the people who need what you offer most—and the good news is, you don't have to start from scratch. In fact, when you've done the work to narrow your focus, marketing becomes exponentially easier. Why? Because now you're not trying to appeal to everyone—you're building bridges to the right people through the right channels.

Niches and Defined Target Audiences Translates into Low Effort, High Return Outreach

This exercise isn't just intended to help you structure your intensive. It's also key to marketing your intensive. Don't panic! I know you entered the mental health field to help people, not to hound people. That's not what this is about. A clearly defined niche paired with a target audience becomes the elevator pitch you need to set yourself apart in everyday interactions that translate into intensive applications.

Referral Partners: When you tell a colleague, "I specialize in grief," they nod politely. But when you say, "I offer 3-day intensives for newly widowed women who feel stuck after the funeral ends and everyone else goes back to normal," they *remember* you. And when someone walks into their office in exactly that situation, they know who to call.

A clear niche makes you referable, and a specific audience gives your referral partners confidence that you're the best fit.

Online Directories: Put your online directory to work for you, too. Whether you're listed on *Psychology Today, Therapy Den*, or a coaching-specific platform, clarity sets you apart. Instead of being one of 100 "grief therapists," you become the one who helps "adult children grieving a parent" or "divorced men rebuilding after loss." These descriptors don't just help search algorithms—they help clients feel seen before they've even reached out.

Current Clients: At the same time, many of your most aligned clients have a friend, a coworker, or a sister walking through something similar. When they know exactly what kind of intensive you offer, they're more likely to share it. Your niche becomes a story they can retell. And that story travels further than any ad.

When you match a clearly defined intensive with the right audience, your marketing doesn't have to be overwhelming. Start simple (Remember: Build, Measure, Learn). In the next chapter, we'll get into some of the ways you can reach beyond your existing network to build out your marketing strategy. If this feels overwhelming to you, then maybe skip this chapter—that's okay!—and focus on the tools that are easily within your reach. When you're ready,

- **Send a targeted update** to past clients or contacts announcing your new intensive offering
- **Tell your top three referral partners** exactly who the intensive is for and what makes it unique
- **Update your directory profiles** with niche-specific language that aligns with your avatar
- **Create one simple resource or post** on your website that speaks directly to your ideal client's pain point, and link it to your intensive

Now that you have done the hard work of narrowing down your focus, let's take that clarity with us into the development of your marketing strategy.

CHAPTER 6

Marketing The Intensive Method

It might seem obvious, but I'm going to say it anyway: not all of Sheryl's potential clients are actively grieving **and** seeking out grief support right this second. But if Sheryl only focuses on the people who are ready for her help right now, she could be missing out on lots of opportunities to help future clients.

As you devise your marketing strategy, it's important to remember that not everyone is ready to sign up for your services right this minute.[8] In fact, according to marketing guru Chet Holmes, only 3% of your entire target audience of clients is ready to sign up right this minute. Let's say there are 100 people in your target audience of clients. That means only 3 of them are ready to work with you right now.

If you want to grow your mental health practice, it isn't enough to just have an Apply Now button on your website. There are four other categories of people you have to keep in mind.

- 7% of your audience is open to your service, but they probably aren't ready to make a purchase today
- 30% of your audience are not thinking about it right now
- Another 30% of your audience don't "believe" they are interested in your service based on the info they have at-hand.
- And then there's another 30% who are definitely not interested.

This is known as The Buyers Pyramid.

---

8 *https://bigbusinessagency.com/insights/what-is-the-buyers-pyramid*

The Intensive Method Buyers Pyramid

Let's put The Buyers Pyramid into terms related to our services. Pretending that there are 100 potential customers who match your target audience profile up above, there are only 3 who are ready to pull out their wallet and calendar and sign up for your intensive today.

The next 7 people know they have a problem to solve, but they're in research mode right now—they are the "tire kickers" on the lot of a car dealership. They've been digging into different options for mental health support and are wondering if intensives are right for them, but probably they aren't ready to sign up for something today.

The next 30 people aren't thinking about intensive therapy right now. They might not know that intensive therapy is a thing. They probably are familiar with traditional therapy options, and down the road, if they hear about an intensive or if their situation changes, they might buy from you someday.

The next 30 people have heard about intensive therapy but they have all kinds of misconceptions and false information about how an intensive works. With some additional information, a persuasive testimony, or a personal connection, they might change their minds and start to consider an intensive.

Finally, there are those last 30 people who, even though they match your target audience description perfectly, they're just never going to opt into an intensive therapy session.

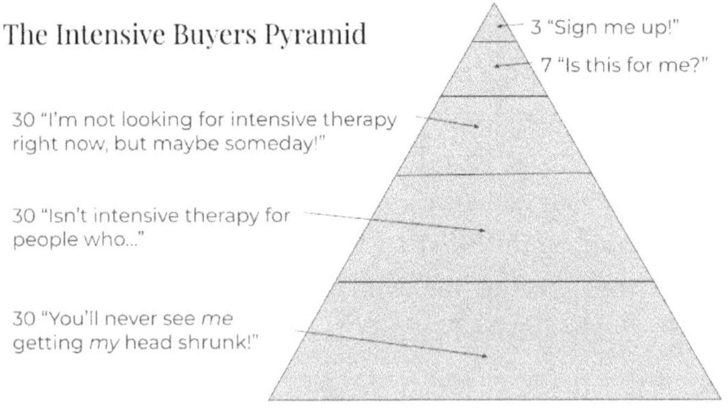

Building Your Sales Funnel

The mistake many businesses make is creating content online and ads out in the world that only pay attention to the needs of the 3%, those people who are ready to buy today.

They don't do anything to draw the attention of those folks who might choose them when the time is right. The content you create to promote your business needs to address the needs of both the person who is ready to buy today *and* the person who might buy from you *someday*.

Essentially, you need to teach the folks who are just sniffing around why your intensive is the obvious choice by offering educational and inspirational content that will help them make a better buying decision when the time comes.

To do this, we're going to build a sales funnel. You will want to build a sales funnel for each of your target audiences you defined in the last chapter. We recommend starting from the bottom of the funnel and working your way up.

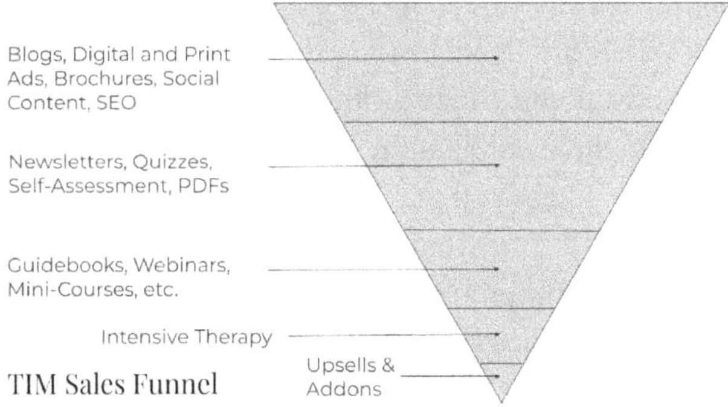

TIM Sales Funnel

Your Core Offer

At the very bottom of your funnel is your core offer, which is your intensive. This is the main thing you want your client to buy on your site. There might be add-ons or upsells later (like additional days of intensive therapy, or group coaching), which you can put at the very tip of the funnel if you'd like, but for the sake of simplicity, we're not going to talk about those right now. We'll cover those possibilities in a later chapter.

You may have the same core offer for all of your target audiences, or you might have a different intensive that is designed specifically for each of your target audiences. In Sheryl's case, her core offer would be her grief intensive for newly widowed women.

Foot-in-the-Door Sale

There will be those few folks (3%) who are ready to buy your core offer today, but there are also those folks who have heard that intensives might be a good option for them. They just aren't ready to go all-in yet. The foot-in-the-door sale (sometimes called a trip wire) is intended to help them make that decision.

A foot-in-the-door sale is just that—a small purchase that serves as a small investment, either financial or time, in exchange for content that will help them in some way. The best foot-in-the-door sales give your potential client enough information to make them realize they might be able to figure this out on their own, but boy, it sure would be helpful if they had a specialist like you to help them through.

Your foot-in-the-door sale might be a guidebook, a webinar, a mini-course, a book, or perhaps even a free session or consultation, which might help them see whether or not an intensive is the right fit for them.

Sheryl might offer a 60-Minute Grief Mapping Call for Widows for somewhere between $49-$99, a private Zoom call to explore the client's feelings, needs, and hopes with a follow-up email that includes a personalized grief care map. To encourage Sheryl's client to enroll in the intensive, she could extend a credit from the session towards her intensive if the client books within 30 days.

In my own practice, I've used some variations of all of these to help our potential clients better understand the problems they are facing and how they could address them... and if they are still struggling, where they can go to get professional help.

Lead Magnet

But what about those folks who aren't ready to make a financial investment? What can you offer to your potential clients who are in the "tire kicking" stage of their search for help but might not be sure if what you offer is even right for them?

A lead magnet is an offering that a client can access in exchange for their contact information, the most obvious being their email address. The best lead magnets serve two purposes: they give your potential client new, helpful information and show them how you can help them with their issues.

This could be a downloadable PDF, an interactive quiz, a self-assessment, a worksheet, a newsletter, or some other kind of content that will help your client begin to address one of the problems that drove them to your site in the first place.

Give away some kind of content that is of value to your target audience in exchange for their contact information, so that you can stay connected with them and promote your core offer—the intensive.

Sheryl might offer a 2-3 page downloadable PDF, "The Early Days of Widowhood: A Gentle Guide for When Everything Feels Upside Down," which any of Sheryl's potential clients can access in exchange for their email address. This PDF achieves two key objectives: it establishes empathy by showing that Sheryl understands the needs of her target audience and it builds credibility by providing simple, effective tools the client can use to begin their healing. Crucially, it also offers a next step for her potential clients, a short section that shares about how intensive grief work can help and where they need to go to learn more.

Both the lead magnet and the foot-in-the-door sale are considered middle-of-the-funnel content. But how do they find this material in the first place?

Top-of-the-Funnel Content

The top of your funnel is where the strategies that attract your audience to your content exist.

What will you do to attract your audience's attention? Think about social media opportunities, online or print ads, places they're doing business, and places they're hanging out as possible outlets for promoting your intensives. What can you be saying to them or sharing with them that might entice them to click and land on your website? Share success stories, testimonials, and other educational content about intensive therapy, especially as it relates to your potential client's challenges.

The key to your top-of-the-funnel content is remembering that only 3% of your target audience are ready to buy today. If you promote a couples therapy intensive on social media, you might get some clicks, but if you promote instead "take this quiz to find out how healthy your marriage is," you're likely to get a lot more engagement, which will ultimately turn into a lot more leads and then a lot more actual clients.

In Sheryl's case, she might write a brief article for her website with a compelling title, like, "What No One Tells You About Grieving the Loss of a Spouse." The article validates her client's feelings, addresses their main pain points, and introduces the idea that there are ways to process and honor this unique experience of grief. It then ends with a gentle call to action that guides them to download the lead magnet for more information.

Where Are Your Customers?

The top of the funnel needs to keep in mind three components:

- Targeting (Who you're addressing)
- Messaging (What they need to hear)
- Strategy (Where you're saying it)

Look back at your target audiences and think about where they're spending their time. You might love to watch videos online, but if your target audience is an older demographic, you probably aren't going to have as much engagement on TikTok (although there are those rare elderly outliers!). If you want to reach Gen Z, probably the only reason they post on Facebook is to connect with their grandparents.

Research your target audience's online habits (a quick online search can go a long way here) to help guide how you spend your time and energy online.

Moving through the Funnel

You want the messaging at each stage of your client's journey to guide them through baby steps to the next point in the sales funnel. Remember, there might be some people who are ready to apply to your intensive today, but it's probably only 3% of all of your target audience.

Think about the first time your potential client interacts with your ad, social media content, or website as if it is a first date. You wouldn't propose to someone on a first date, right? Sure, there are tales of first date proposals out there in the world, but most of the time, people need time to get to know each other before they're ready to make that next leap. Maybe after the third coffee date—after you've exchanged phone numbers, say—they are ready to spend a whole evening with you, eating dinner and going to a movie.

Eventually, it'll be time to pop the question... will you please apply for my intensive?! Sometimes, your target audience will shop for weeks, months, or even years before they are ready to reach out for help. Often the items or services that are the most expensive will have a longer nurture period and require a more personalized approach. That's where your application, consultation calls, and screening calls come in. We'll talk more about those in Part 4.

In addition to a complete, top-to-bottom sales funnel, there needs to be some hand-holds along the way to help your potential client move through the funnel. Once they've downloaded your lead magnet, you don't want to leave it up to them to reach back out to you. Send a follow-up email asking if they had any questions. Send another that offers them another piece of content (like your foot-in-the-door sale). Help them see what their next step is, and then give them clear instructions on how to take that next step.

Strategize, Simplify, Systemize

You might have lots and lots of ideas for lead magnets, lots and lots of ideas for mini-courses, and lots and lots of ideas for different intensives you can offer. Ideas are great! But they can also be overwhelming to the point of paralysis. Keep your sales funnel super simple to begin with. Remember, the goal is to get to a Minimum Viable Product, and then Build, Measure, and Learn! In the meantime, put all of those other ideas on a future list of "stuff to try out" later. Once you have a sales funnel up and running, you can always tweak and add new messaging, lead magnets, and foot-in-the-door options to try out alongside your existing funnel or in place of strategies that didn't work as well as you hoped.

There are also a lot of different systems you can invest in to make marketing easier, including social media schedulers, automated emails to guide your potential clients from one step of the funnel to the next, and more.[9]

Ultimately, I know you aren't here to become a marketing expert, but understanding these principles can help you find and hire the right partners who *can* support your intensive practice and avoid investing thousands of dollars in practices that won't lead to clients. If all of this feels overwhelming, remember to *keep it simple* and *start small.*

As you begin connecting your intensive offering with the people who need it most, each step—from your referral conversations to your directory listings to your lead magnet—builds momentum.

But the most effective marketing strategies don't just tell people what you offer; they tell people who you are. That's where your brand identity comes in. Your

9 *Several worksheets for target audience and sales funnel development are available for download on our website and explored in-depth through The Intensive Method online course.*

brand is more than a logo or a tagline—it's the emotional imprint you leave, the tone of your voice, and the values that guide your work. In the next chapter, we'll explore how to shape a brand identity that reflects your strengths, resonates with your audience, and positions your intensives with clarity and authenticity.

CHAPTER 7

Developing Your Brand Identity

Now that you've defined your target audiences and begun to consider how you will reach the right people in the right places, it's time to sharpen and hone the messaging that will resonate with your target audience.

It's entirely possible that intensive counseling or coaching services will fit snugly into your existing brand identity. If the target audiences you've defined are very similar to the people you're already serving, then intensives are just one more "product" or "offering" in your collection of services you already provide.

Even if this is the case, it doesn't hurt to zoom out and evaluate just what your branding says about who you are and what you do.

A strong brand identity provides the following for organizations like yours:

Clarity: Establishing these elements provides clarity about the purpose and direction of the business. It helps stakeholders, including clients, practitioners, and employees, understand what the business stands for and what it aims to achieve.

If your materials promote "counseling services," but you really only provide counseling for couples in crisis, then your potential clients might feel like they've wasted a lot of time browsing your website only to realize you don't suit their needs. A general "counseling services" umbrella can also waste you and your staff's time fielding calls for clients whose needs you can't meet.

On the other hand, if your brand overemphasizes one major area of service, then you could be missing out on a target demographic that might benefit from your services. For example, maybe your counseling team specializes in addiction counseling, but all of the images on your site are of old, white men. This branding might appeal to old, white men, but women, younger individuals, and people of color won't necessarily see themselves reflected in your material and assume that you are out of touch with their needs.

Defining your brand identity provides clarity, for you, for your team, and for your target audience.

Consistency: Having a clearly defined brand identity, mission, vision, and values ensures consistency in messaging and actions. Consistency builds trust and credibility with clients and other stakeholders.

Attracting Clients: A well-defined brand identity and mission statement can attract clients who resonate with the values and goals of the therapy business. People seeking therapy often look for services that align with their own beliefs and values. It can be tempting to broaden and generalize your brand identity with the hopes of being "all things to all people," but as I've said before, the "riches are in the niches." The better you can define who you are and what you believe in, the more likely you are to reach clients who resonate with your values.

Employee Engagement: Clearly communicated values and a compelling mission can help attract and retain talented practitioners and staff who are passionate about the business's purpose. When employees feel connected to the mission and values, they are more engaged and motivated in their work.

Competitive Advantage: A distinct brand identity sets a therapy business apart from competitors. It helps differentiate the business in a crowded market and can attract clients who are seeking a unique or specialized approach to therapy.

Guiding Decision-Making: A well-defined mission and set of values serve as a guide for decision-making within the business. They help ensure that actions and initiatives are aligned with the overarching goals and principles of the organization.

Building Trust: Clearly articulated values and a strong brand identity help build trust with clients. Trust is essential in the therapeutic relationship, and a consistent brand identity communicates reliability and professionalism.

Defining Your Brand Identity Begins with You

So, where do you begin? Begin with you. You are the one who is setting the course for this business, so the best place to start is with your own personal values, mission, and vision.[10] Defining your brand identity will help guide your entire business for years to come. This activity is worth your energy and extended attention.

Your Values

Think about your personal values. Reflecting on personal values is an essential step for therapists and coaches to understand themselves better and how these values influence their professional practice. Consider the following questions:

Why did you choose to become a mental health practitioner? Reflect on the motivations that led you to pursue a career in therapy. What aspects of the profession attracted you?

What are the core principles that guide your life? Identify the fundamental beliefs and principles that shape your decisions and actions in both personal and professional contexts.

What experiences have shaped your values? Consider significant life experiences, relationships, and challenges that have influenced the development of your values.

What do you believe about the nature of human beings and their capacity for change? Explore your beliefs about human nature, resilience, and the potential for growth and transformation.

How do you define success in your personal and professional life? Reflect on what success means to you and how it aligns with your values and aspirations.

What do you prioritize in your relationships with others? Consider the values that underpin your interactions and relationships with clients, colleagues, and others in your life.

What role do compassion and empathy play in your work? Reflect on the importance of compassion, empathy, and connection in your practice's relation-

---

10 Brand Identity Worksheets are included in The Intensive Method online course and are also available for download at theintensivemethod.com.

ships and interactions.

How do you approach ethical dilemmas and decision-making? Consider how your values inform your approach to ethical dilemmas and decision-making in your professional practice.

What impact do you want to have on the lives of your clients? Reflect on the goals and aspirations you have for your clients and the kind of impact you hope to make through your work.

How do you maintain balance and well-being in your own life? Consider how your values influence the choices you make to maintain balance, self-care, and well-being in your personal and professional life.

Spend some time meditating on and journaling through these questions. Once you've done that work, you can start building out your core values. Here's how:

Identify Common Themes: Review the responses to the reflective questions and identify common themes or recurring values that stand out. These could include compassion, empathy, integrity, respect for diversity, commitment to growth, etc.

Articulate Core Values: Based on the identified themes, articulate a set of core values that represent the practitioner's beliefs, principles, and priorities. These values should reflect what is most important to them both personally and professionally.

Translate Values into Statements: Translate each core value into a concise, clear statement that communicates its meaning and significance. For example:

Core Value: *Compassion*

Statement: *"We demonstrate compassion by actively listening, empathizing, and providing nonjudgmental support to our clients."*

Core Value: *Integrity*

Statement: *"We uphold the highest ethical standards and honesty in our interactions with clients, colleagues, and the community."*

Clarify Your Mission

Even though often the mission statement for an organization is the overarching signpost that defines who you are and what you do, it is built on the foundation of your core values. Now that you've articulated your core values, let's take a closer look at writing your mission statement.

Your mission statement should define the purpose of your practice. What is your reason for being in this profession? How do you want to serve your clients? Your mission statement should succinctly capture the essence of your practice's goals and intentions.

Start by reflecting on your personal purpose as a practitioner and the value statements you've drafted. Think about what sets your practice apart from others. Consider your unique skills, experiences, and areas of expertise that you bring to your work. You've done some work already to define your target audience. Use that material in your mission statement. Your mission statement should reflect your commitment to addressing these needs and providing value to your clients. Consider the benefits that clients derive from your therapy services. How do you help them? What positive outcomes do you aim to facilitate? Think about the impact you want to have on your clients, your community, and the field of mental health as a whole. Your mission statement should convey your aspirations for creating positive change and making a difference.

Craft a mission statement that is clear, concise, and easy to understand. Avoid jargon or overly complex language. Your mission statement should be accessible to clients and resonate with them on a personal level. It should also inspire both you and your clients, conveying a sense of purpose, passion, and commitment to your work. Once you have drafted your mission statement, seek feedback from colleagues, mentors, or trusted friends. They can provide valuable insights and suggestions for improvement.

Review your mission statement periodically and revise it as needed to ensure that it remains relevant and reflective of your evolving practice and goals.

Here is our Intensive Method Mission Statement as an example: "Our mission is to spark a journey of accelerated healing and profound personal growth for clients while empowering clinical professionals in mental health roles to transcend conventional boundaries of counseling and coaching."

Cast Vision

While your mission statement defines who you are and what you do, a vision statement points you in the direction you want to go. When you're working on your vision statement, you're trying to envision the future of your practice. What do you hope to achieve? How do you see your practice evolving over time? Think about the impact you want to make on your clients and the broader community.

A vision statement helps you stay the course as the leader of the organization. It gives your organization and staff purpose and meaning, a destination and a goal they are working to achieve together. For clients, a vision statement communicates the type of experience they can expect from your practice in the long term. It provides them with a sense of what the practice aims to accomplish and how it will benefit them.

A vision statement also communicates your commitment to serving the community and collaborating with other professionals in the field. It can attract referrals from other healthcare providers and community organizations who share similar goals and values. A compelling vision can also position the practice as a leader in the community and foster partnerships that enhance its impact and reach. And finally, a vision statement can demonstrate the practice's commitment to quality, innovation, and ethical standards to regulatory bodies and accrediting agencies.

Drafting Your Vision Statement

Use the following journaling questions to think through your long-term goals, aspirations, and hopes for your business.

What are the ideal outcomes and achievements that your practice aims to accomplish over time?

How does your vision statement speak to different stakeholders, including your clients, your team, and your peers?

What are the overarching goals and aspirations your practice aims to achieve in the future? These goals should be ambitious yet realistic, reflecting your vision for the practice's growth and impact.

Your vision statement should inspire and motivate both internal and external stakeholders. Use language that evokes a sense of purpose, passion, and possibility, encouraging others to rally behind the vision.

Here is The Intensive Method's Vision Statement: "We envision a world where mental health treatment is not only more effective but also more efficient, where individuals, couples, and families receive the support they need to thrive, and practitioners are equipped with practical tools and greater flexibility to deliver impactful care with lasting results. Through the catalytic launch of The Intensive Method, we aim to pioneer a new era in clinical practices around the globe, transforming lives one intensive session at a time."

Building Your Brand Visuals

With both your target audiences defined and your mission, vision, and values in place, you have all of the necessary tools to build your brand visuals. You can always hire a branding consultant or marketing agency to help you come up with the logo, colors, fonts, visual identity, and tone of voice, but only you can define those larger elements that shape your brand.

We recommend consulting with an outside agency to help you shape the visual identity of your brand. Here are some reasons why defining your brand is important:

Professionalism and Credibility: Consistent visual branding conveys professionalism and credibility to clients and stakeholders. It establishes the practitioner as a reputable and trustworthy professional in the mental health field, instilling confidence in potential clients.

Brand Recognition: Consistent visual branding helps practitioners create a strong and recognizable brand identity. When clients encounter consistent branding across various touchpoints, such as the practitioner's website, social media profiles, and marketing materials, they are more likely to remember and recognize the practitioner's practice.

Differentiation: In a crowded market, consistent visual branding helps practitioners differentiate their practice from competitors. By establishing a distinct visual identity, practitioners can stand out and attract clients who resonate with their brand values and offerings.

Professionalism and Consistency: Ensure that all visual elements, including logos, colors, fonts, and imagery, are cohesive and aligned with your brand identity. Consistency in visual branding creates a unified and polished appearance that reflects positively on the practitioner's professionalism and attention to detail.

Client Experience: Consistent visual branding contributes to a cohesive and memorable client experience. When clients encounter consistent branding at every touchpoint, from initial contact to ongoing communication, they feel more connected to your practice and perceive it as reliable and trustworthy.

Builds Trust and Loyalty: A consistent visual brand builds trust and fosters loyalty among clients. When clients encounter consistent branding over time, they develop a sense of familiarity and reliability with the practitioner's practice, leading to stronger relationships and repeat business.

Ease of Communication: Consistent visual branding simplifies communication with clients and stakeholders. Clients can easily recognize and identify the practitioner's practice across various platforms, making it easier for them to engage with your services and refer others to the practice.

Supports Marketing Efforts: Consistent visual branding supports marketing efforts by providing a cohesive framework for promotional materials and campaigns. Whether online or offline, you can leverage consistent branding to create impactful marketing materials that resonate with your target audience.

Writing Your Brand's Story

Part of effective marketing involves developing a compelling and consistent brand story that emphasizes the positive impact of intensives. We're especially fond of the StoryBrand concept, developed by Donald Miller, which positions your client as the hero of a story, and the practitioner as the guide who helps the hero achieve their goals.[11]

The hero / guide concept flips the narrative that organizations typically try to tell into a more compelling story, one that your clients can relate to. Many businesses like to tell the story of their practice, leading with credentials, years in business, and therapeutic techniques. This information is important, but what matters most to a client right now is the pain they are in and how you might be able to help them.

Writing your brand's story in this way directs the creation of all of your other marketing content, from your website to your social media to brochures and everything in between.[12]

---

11 *https://storybrand.com/*

12 *Worksheets to help you compose your brand story are available to download at theintensivemethod.com and through The Intensive Method online course.*

It will take some time and energy to put together your 10,000 foot view of your intensive services, but trust me, this work is so worth it! Once you've defined your brand identity, you will have so much more clarity and direction for future marketing efforts, which we'll get into in even greater detail (did you even think that was possible?!) in the next chapter.

CHAPTER 8

Shaping Your Comprehensive Marketing Plan

In the previous chapters, we've covered together many of the key components of marketing that will help you be successful when you are ready to launch your intensive practice. But there are still a few more elements that can really set your practice apart and help convert potential clients into raving fans of your work.

Customer Testimonials

Customer testimonials play an important part in your marketing strategy. There are several psychological reasons why testimonials are so effective. Testimonials provide evidence that others have benefited from a service, which makes prospective clients more likely to trust and choose a service for themselves. Testimonials from real clients enhance the credibility of a service provider by acting as third-party endorsements, which are more trusted than self-promotional content (even when your self-promotional content is super sharp and professional).

Seeking mental health support can be a daunting decision filled with uncertainty. Testimonials can alleviate some of this uncertainty by providing reassurance that others have had positive outcomes. It's also important to note that when potential clients read testimonials, they often see reflections of their own problems and aspirations in the stories of others. This relatability can help potential clients feel understood. If these other people feel supported and encouraged, maybe you can help them as well. These testimonials also evoke emotions, creating a personal connection with the reader, which makes the marketing message more memorable and persuasive, encouraging potential clients to take action.

Testimonials, especially from respected individuals or those perceived as authorities, can significantly influence potential clients' decisions. Authority figures' endorsements can lend additional weight and credibility to your services, further persuading potential clients.

Incorporating testimonials into marketing leverages these psychological principles to build trust, reduce uncertainty, and emotionally engage potential clients, ultimately increasing the likelihood of them choosing your services.

Enhancing Your Marketing Strategy

Reviews and testimonials from your clients won't do you any good if they just sit in the database after they've submitted them to you. There are many ways you can use client testimonials to enhance your marketing efforts. You might want to flesh out the Sales Funnel for each of your target audiences with these ideas. Some of these require a little more leg work than others, but they're worth the effort:

Website Testimonials Page: Your website is your practice's virtual storefront. It's the place your prospective clients go to gauge whether you are really someone they're willing to trust and work with. Create a dedicated section on your website to showcase client testimonials. Be sure to respect your client's wishes in terms of anonymity—you can always use initials or first names only when you're quoting their experiences.

Social Media Sharing: Testimonials can really boost your engagement on social media as well. Share positive testimonials on social media platforms like Facebook, Instagram, and LinkedIn. Use visually appealing graphics or videos to make these posts more engaging.

Google and Yelp Reviews: As part of your evaluation process, you might consider setting up an auto-reply to survey respondents that thanks them for their feedback and invites them to leave reviews on platforms like Google My Business and Yelp. Positive reviews on these sites can significantly enhance your online reputation and attract new clients. Use discretion with this one: there may be some intensives that deal with sensitive subject-matter that a client might feel uncomfortable reviewing publicly.

Email Newsletters: Circle back to your sales funnel and email nurture sequences to sprinkle client testimonials into your emails and newsletters. These will help build trust with your audience. Highlighting success stories can encourage potential clients to seek your services.

Brochures and Fliers: Incorporate testimonials into your printed marketing materials. This can be particularly effective for distributing at local events, clinics, or other community gatherings.

Video Testimonials: If you have a client who is very passionate about the experiences they've had working with you, they might make a great candidate for a video testimonial. Short videos featuring client testimonials can be more persuasive than text alone and can be shared on your website, social media, and YouTube channel. Just as with any client information, you will need to take appropriate steps to make sure your client is well-informed about how their video will be used, aware of confidentiality considerations, and given the opportunity to remain anonymous or use a pseudonym to protect their identity in the video. To protect yourself, obtain written consent from your client and check HIPAA and other local regulations regarding the sharing of personal health details. Video testimonials should benefit the client, not cause them additional harm. Keep your client's well-being in mind throughout the process.

SEO and Blog Content: Use testimonials within blog posts on your website to improve SEO and provide real-life examples of how your services have helped others. This content can attract more traffic and build credibility.

Client Success Stories: A short testimonial from one of your evaluations could be the beginning of a more in-depth article or blog post featuring a client's success story. You might interview a client to highlight the challenges they faced and their personal experience and then enhance the post with more clinical details about the therapy process and the outcomes achieved.

Professional Listings and Directories: Include testimonials in your profiles on professional directories and listing websites. This can help potential clients decide to contact you over other practitioners.

Workshops and Seminars: If you present any workshops or seminars, you can share anonymized client success stories to illustrate the effectiveness of your methods and build credibility with participants.

Advertising Campaigns: Use testimonials in your online and offline advertising campaigns. Positive client experiences can significantly enhance the impact of your ads. As a reminder, when using client testimonials and feedback, always ensure you have their explicit permission to use their comments publicly, and respect their privacy by anonymizing their information if necessary.

Building a Referral Network

You can further elevate your intensive practice by building a referral network for your organization. Just like testimonials, referrals are a powerful approach to building your practice. Here are some steps to consider to establish and leverage a referral system for your practice:

Identify Potential Referral Sources: These might include professional contacts who might refer clients needing intensive therapy to you; medical professionals who might have patients requiring intensive mental health care; community organizations like schools, support groups, religious organizations, or community centers; and current and former clients who might refer family, friends, and acquaintances. Other counselors or coaches would make excellent potential partners, especially those who do not have any interest in offering intensives themselves but see the value of intensives for their clients.

Build Relationships: If you don't feel like you have much of a network yet, you might need to start and nurture relationships through professional conferences, local health fairs, and community events. Or, perhaps you can develop formal or informal partnerships with other professionals. In either case, you want to nurture that relationship through regular updates, newsletters, or casual check-ins.

Create a Referral Program: A professional referral program needs to have clear guidelines about who qualifies and what services you offer so that your potential referrers understand the types of clients you are best suited to help. You might want to offer referral incentives, like several ready-to-go gifts, to recognize a person for their referral. This is a great option for coaches. Try to make the referral process as simple as possible with an easy-to-use referral form on your website, or provide a direct contact person who can handle referrals promptly.

Educate Your Referrers: Make sure that you provide your referrers with informative materials they can share with potential clients. You might also want to host information sessions for potential referrers so you can educate them about your practice and how it could benefit their clients.

Leverage Client Testimonials: This is yet another way you can use your client testimonials to boost your practice! Share anonymized success stories and testimonials with potential referrers to further underscore the effectiveness of your practice.

Promote Your Referral Program: Send out emails to your professional contacts and promote your program through networking events, professional meetings, and consultations to establish solid referral partnerships with individuals you can trust.

Maintain and Nurture Relationships: Once your referral program is established, you don't want to just set it and forget it. Follow up with your referrers periodically to maintain relationships and express appreciation. Implement a feedback loop about the referral process so that you know how you can improve your system.

Track Referrals: You want to be able to gauge the effectiveness of your system and track where your referrals are coming from. You can do this through a simple spreadsheet or CRM system.

By developing a structured referral system and fostering strong professional relationships, you can build a steady stream of new clients for your intensive practice while ensuring those clients receive high-quality care.

Ongoing Marketing Strategies

As your intensive practice begins to pick up steam, regularly revisit your marketing strategy, sales funnels, and so on. Remember, you don't have to do everything, but you want to be doing something at each level of your sales funnel—top, middle, and bottom. Don't hesitate to make adjustments to your marketing strategy as you go along. Try new things from time to time—you might be surprised to find out that your clients love quizzes but don't seem that interested in free downloads. Stay nimble and creative.

There are so many things that you can do, but at the least, you will want to make sure you have these core elements in place:

Professional Online Presence: Create a website that is professional and user friendly, and optimize it for search engines with relevant keywords.

Email Marketing: Your email list is yours. Collect email addresses from your website visitors and social media followers to regularly communicate with people. You might consider starting a regular newsletter to share updates about your services, pro tips, relevant news or research, and inspirational recommendations to support their mental health journey.

Social Media: Many customers who don't know you yet may find you on social media. Share informative content related to mental health, therapy techniques, and success stories. You want your social media to be less of a sales pitch and more of an educational/informational space that your clients and prospective clients will find engaging and entertaining.

When you put all of the material together from these last four chapters, you'll have yourself a comprehensive marketing plan. Way to go!

We have just one more subject to cover before we wrap up Part 2, and that's packaging and pricing your intensive. This final chapter regarding marketing your intensive will help you pitch your services with confidence.

CHAPTER 9

Packaging, Pricing, and Profit

Now that you've clarified your niche, defined your target audience, articulated what makes your brand distinct, and considered various marketing strategies, it's time to bring it all together in the heart of your business: **your core offer.**

Your intensive is more than a service, it's a transformation you're guiding someone through, and the way you package that experience—how you structure it, describe it, price it, and deliver it—can make the difference between occasional interest and a sustainable, thriving practice. In this last chapter on marketing, we'll walk through how to align your client's needs with the intensive you offer, while making sure that this program supports your income goals and professional boundaries.

Align Your Client's Needs with Your Intensive Offering

Take a moment to revisit the work you did earlier in Part 2 to define your target audience. Now is a good time to start brainstorming what your intensive core offer could look like for each target audience. Find their primary need and then make a list of the various therapies and techniques you think would be beneficial to help them address that need.

You can probably identify two to three major needs people have when they come to you for help. Align the title and description of your intensive with the challenges they are facing so that it is very clear what they will get out of your intensive experience.[13]

With these out-of-the-box intensives in place for each of your target audiences, you can improvise and adjust to accommodate the particular needs of each of your clients without having to start a treatment plan from scratch each time.

Writing Promotional Content for Your Intensives

Whether you're assembling a brochure or a webpage of content about your intensive, the same basic principles apply. If you follow this general framework, you should be able to generate content for your website or promotional material. Remember to use client sensitive language, not something overly clinical to market towards your ideal avatar. Repeat this structure for each of your intensive offerings or target audiences:[14]

Introduction: Start with a captivating headline that grabs attention and highlights the unique benefits of your intensive program. What is this program about and how will it help the person who just landed on your page? What pain are they moving away from? In the next section, introduce your practice or organization briefly, emphasizing your expertise, commitment to client care, and the transformative potential of your intensive services.

Overview of Intensives: Provide a brief overview of what an intensive entails, emphasizing the concentrated and immersive nature of the experience. Highlight the advantages of intensives, such as accelerated progress, deeper insights, and lasting change compared to traditional mental health service formats.

Key Features and Benefits: Outline the key features of your intensive program, including duration, format, and any additional services or amenities offered. Highlight the benefits clients can expect to gain from participating in the program, such as enhanced self-awareness, improved coping skills, and greater emotional resilience. Try to keep this list between

---

13 *Worksheets to support this process are available for download at theintensivemethod.com or through The Intensive Method online course.*

14 *A Web Content Structure for Intensive Promotion worksheet is available for download at theintensivemethod.com and through The Intensive Method online course.*

five and seven succinct bullet points.

Customization and Personalization: Emphasize your commitment to personalized care and the customization of treatment plans to meet each client's unique needs, goals, and preferences.

Therapeutic Approach and Expertise: Describe the therapeutic approach or modalities used in your intensive program, highlighting their evidence-based nature and effectiveness in addressing a range of mental health concerns. Showcase the qualifications, experience, and specialization of your therapists or practitioners, emphasizing their expertise in delivering intensive services.

Packaging Options and Additional Services: Provide details about the different packaging options available, such as services or optional amenities that will enhance their experience. You might also list here any specialized programs or tailored tracks within the intensive program.

Client Testimonials and Success Stories: As a reminder, other people's stories persuade people who are on the fence about reaching out to take that step, so make sure you include testimonials or quotes from past clients who have benefited from your intensive program, showcasing their positive experiences and outcomes. Remember if you ask for post-intensive evaluations, put a note on your evaluation form asking for permission to use positive comments anonymously as future testimonials and marketing materials. This way you have both content and permission in the same place.

Application Information: Provide instructions or a call to action to apply for your intensive. I do not recommend listing the price of your services on your website. You can go over these details on your screening call, after a client has taken the time to go through the application process.

Contact Information and Next Steps: Include your contact details prominently, inviting potential clients to reach out with any questions or to schedule a consultation. Encourage interested individuals to take the next step towards their mental health and well-being by participating in your intensive program.

This content flow provides your client with a clear understanding of your intensive and the steps required to begin working with you.

What an incredible service you provide! But... how much does it cost?

How to Price Your Intensive

Once you have a clear idea of your target audience and what your client can expect from your intensive, it's time to figure out your fee structure. The nature of an intensive and part of its draw is that it provides you with the opportunity to increase revenue above doing regular hourly sessions.

Pricing should reflect the value, expertise, and outcomes delivered to clients during intensive therapy sessions. There are several factors to consider when pricing your intensive:

Market Rates: Research the rates charged by other practitioners in your area for similar intensive programs. This will give you a baseline understanding of what clients may be willing to pay.

Expertise and Experience: Consider your level of expertise, qualifications, and experience as a mental health practitioner. Higher levels of expertise may justify higher pricing.

Session Duration and Frequency: Determine the duration and frequency of your intensives. For simplicity, we're going to talk specifically about 3-day intensives.

Value of Services Provided: Assess the value of the services provided within the intensive therapy program. This includes factors such as personalized treatment plans, additional resources, follow-up support, and the overall impact on clients' lives.

Overhead Costs: Take into account any overhead costs associated with running the intensive program. For many people, there is no additional cost, but if there is, you would want to consider things like rent, materials, administrative expenses, and marketing efforts.

Client Demographics: Consider the demographics and financial means of your target client base. Adjust your pricing accordingly to ensure it is accessible to your desired clientele while still reflecting the value of your services.

Profit Margin: Determine the profit margin you aim to achieve from each intensive session. This will depend on your financial goals and the sustainability of your practice.

Discounts and Packages: Decide whether you will offer discounts for clients who commit to multiple sessions or who pay upfront for a package deal. This can incentivize clients to invest in your intensive programs while also maximizing your revenue.

Flexibility: Remain flexible in your pricing approach. You may need to adjust your rates over time based on changes in market demand, competition, or your own professional development. Most commonly, people increase their rates over time, not decrease them.

Client Feedback: Solicit feedback from clients who have participated in your intensive programs to gauge their perceived value and satisfaction with the pricing. This feedback can help you refine your pricing strategy in the future. While there will always be people who will complain about things being too expensive, there is something to be said for clients being willing to have skin in the game. So be sure you do not underprice your intensives either.

Intensive Fees

Let's talk about the value of services provided, session duration and frequency, and your expertise and experience for a minute. The nature of intensives requires a higher level of commitment and a sizable chunk of your time. The concentrated time, schedule, and intensity warrant an additional fee above and beyond the cost of your typical clinical hours. It is a value-add to your client who is paying for both your expertise and your singular focus on their lives for three full days (and then some, with aftercare included).

Besides time, you are bringing a higher degree of expertise and experience into the intensive setting. If you have additional credentials, certifications, or specializations, these professional designations warrant an increase in fees for advanced treatment options. These additional fees are above and beyond your typical clinical hourly fee rate, which is why intensives are such a great model for therapists who are able to deliver this concentrated form of therapy.

3-Day Intensive, General Fee Grid

Clinician	Base Therapy Fee	3-Day Intensive Fee	
Hourly Rate	3 Days - 6 Hours per Day	Basic Level Clinician/Specialty	Total Intensive Cost
$100	$1,800	$1,800	$3,600
$125	$2,250	$1,800	$4,050
$150	$2,700	$1,800	$4,500
$175	$3,150	$1,800	$4,950
$200	$3,600	$1,800	$5,400
$225	$4,050	$1,800	$5,850
$250	$4,500	$1,800	$6,300
$275	$4,950	$1,800	$6,750
$300	$5,400	$1,800	$7,200
$325	$5,850	$1,800	$7,650
$350	$6,300	$1,800	$8,100
$375	$6,750	$1,800	$8,550
$400	$7,200	$1,800	$9,000
$425	$7,650	$1,800	$9,450
$450	$8,100	$1,800	$9,900
$475	$8,550	$1,800	$10,350
$500	$9,000	$1,800	$10,800

Additional fee grids are included with the Fee Structure Questionnaire & Calculator at theintensivemethod.com.

For some of you, The Intensive Method is an option to increase revenue because you simply need a higher level of income. For others, perhaps you wish you had more time in life for other things. Maybe you'd like to be more available to serve underserved populations or potential clients who simply cannot afford treatment, and the increased revenue will allow more flexibility to serve those clients. In any of those situations or others we haven't mentioned, The Intensive Method provides opportunities for clinicians to increase their revenue goals by working smarter, not harder.

To determine what rate you should charge for your intensive, you need to begin by addressing your personal financial goals. Take a moment to answer these questions:

1. **What is your current hourly rate?**
2. **How many hours do you currently average per week in therapy sessions?**
3. **How much revenue do you lose weekly due to insurance (if in network)?**
4. **How much do you desire to make per year?**
5. **How many weeks off do you want each year?**
6. **How many 3-day intensives would you like to do a month?**

Take the answers to the first three questions to calculate your current typical income each week.

Typical Income Per Week =
current hourly rate * average hours of therapy - insurance

Then, determine how many weeks you want to take off each year for vacation:

Typical Gross Annual Income = weekly income * (52 - vacation weeks)

Now, with your answers to the rest of the questions above, let's dream together! We've created a Fee Calculator[15] that can help you with these calculations so you can see in real-time what your revenue could be, but here's a snapshot scenario:

---

15 A Fee Structure Questionnaire and Calculator is available for download at theintensivemethod.com and through The Intensive Method online course.

Current Practice Outcomes	
Current Hourly Rate:	$150
Current Average Therapy Hours Per Week:	40
How much revenue do you lose weekly due to insurance (if in network):	$1,000
Typical Income Per Week:	**$5,000**
How many weeks you take off each year:	4
Typical Gross Annual Income:	**$240,000**
Your Dream Financial Goals	
How much do you desire to make per year?	$300,000
How many weeks off do you want each year?	6
How many 3-day intensives would you like to do a month?	2
3-Day Intensives Per Year:	**24**
# of Additional Aftercare Days Per Year (2 per 3-day intensive):	**48**
Projected Income with General Intensives:	**$165,600**
Projected Income Inclusive of Regular Practice:	**$275,600**
Advanced Clinician or Special Certification Projected Income:	**$213,600**
Projected Income Inclusive of Regular Practice w/ Adv. Clinician:	**$323,600**

Keep in mind that a 3-day intensive is **18** clinical hours, and the two aftercare days add up to **12** clinical hours, which means you only work **30** hours in a typical intensive-based week of work. You certainly can adjunctively add traditional hours that week if you want, but one of the gifts of this method is the guaranteed clinical hours per client.

The rate you can charge for an intensive is going to vary depending on your current clinical hourly rate, but you can also increase your intensive fees if you have advanced training or special certification.

If you have any of these additional advanced training or certifications, you might consider increasing your intensive fee:

Specialized Therapy Modalities: Advanced training in specialized therapy modalities such as Cognitive Behavioral Therapy (CBT), Dialectical Behavior Therapy (DBT), Eye Movement Desensitization and

Reprocessing (EMDR), Acceptance and Commitment Therapy (ACT), or Schema Therapy can demonstrate expertise in specific areas of treatment.

Trauma-Informed Care Certification: Certification in trauma-informed care equips practitioners with the skills to work effectively with individuals who have experienced trauma, which is valuable for intensive therapy programs focusing on trauma recovery.

Certified Substance Abuse Counselor (CSAC): Becoming a CSAC demonstrates expertise in treating substance abuse and addiction, which may be relevant for intensive therapy programs targeting substance use disorders.

Certified Sex Therapist: Certification in sex therapy provides specialized training in addressing sexual health issues and dysfunctions, which may be beneficial for intensive therapy programs focusing on relationships or sexual wellness.

Certified Family Therapist: Advanced training in family therapy can enhance a therapist's ability to work with families and couples, which may be relevant for intensive therapy programs focusing on relationship dynamics or family systems.

Certification in Mindfulness-Based Interventions: Training in mindfulness-based interventions such as Mindfulness-Based Stress Reduction (MBSR) or Mindfulness-Based Cognitive Therapy (MBCT) can enhance a therapist's ability to incorporate mindfulness practices into intensive therapy programs.

Certified Eating Disorder Specialist (CEDS): Certification as an eating disorder specialist demonstrates expertise in treating eating disorders, which may be relevant for intensive therapy programs focusing on disordered eating or body image issues.

Certified Clinical Supervisor: Becoming a certified clinical supervisor allows therapists to supervise and mentor other mental health professionals, which may enhance their reputation and credibility in the field.

Advanced Degrees: Pursuing advanced degrees such as a Ph.D. or Psy.D. in psychology or counseling can demonstrate a therapist's commitment to ongoing education and professional development, which may justify higher fees for intensive therapy services.

Advanced Training in Neuroscience or Psychopharmacology: Training in neuroscience or psychopharmacology can provide therapists with a deeper understanding of the biological basis of mental health disorders and treatment options, which may enhance their ability to provide comprehensive care in intensive therapy programs.

Beyond these considerations, you'll want to factor in the following additional costs when calculating what to charge for your services:

- costs associated with offering intensives, including rent for space, utilities, insurance, licensing fees, marketing expenses, and additional staff or resources
- the time commitment for each intensive, including preparation, session time, and follow-up
- overhead, both direct and indirect (administrative support, office supplies, and technology expenses)
- your specialized training or certifications
- the local market and the market for competing intensives across the country
- the unique value of intensive therapy
- potential discounts for package deals on multiple intensives
- sliding scales for clients with financial constraints
- potential insurance reimbursement
- the cost of no-shows and cancellations

All of these factors will help you come to the appropriate price for the packages of therapy you offer.

If you haven't yet developed your intensive fully, it may be a little premature to set your intensive rate; however, I wanted to give you a vision for what intensives could do for you and your practice financially. For the right clinician, intensives can be both impactful and lucrative! The best way to ensure both is to develop a core offer, aka an intensive, that is clear, compelling, and effective. In Part 3, we'll turn our attention to this most important work, Delivering Effective Intensives.

PART 3

Delivering Effective Intensives

CHAPTER 10

Designing the 3-Day Experience

Designing an intensive is much more than planning a series of extended therapy sessions. A true intensive offers something deeper: a complete and intentional experience. When crafted thoughtfully, an intensive leads a client through an emotional and psychological journey that moves them from **stuck** to **healing**, from **confusion** to **clarity**, from **despair** to **hope**.

At the heart of designing an effective intensive is the recognition that you are not only the therapist, you are also the architect of your client's experience. Every aspect of these three days, from the session flow to the physical environment, contributes to the story your client will live and the transformation they will undergo. You are constructing not just a schedule but a deeply immersive journey, one that must be carefully paced, structured, and stewarded.

Your goal is to construct an experience that maximizes engagement, fosters discovery, and creates lasting change. Clinical techniques are important—and we will turn to those in a later chapter—but they must rest on a solid foundation of strategic experience design.

You are the architect of your client's experience. Besides the therapy they expect to receive during their time with you, an intensive truly is an experience, and you are constructing both the environment and the journey they'll take while they are with you.

One of the most effective frameworks for building a 3-day intensive is to organize the experience around a natural progression through time: the past, the present, and the future. We talked about this a bit in chapter 4. People understand their lives best when they can anchor their story to familiar markers, and helping a client move thoughtfully through their history, their current realities, and their future possibilities allows the therapeutic experience to feel coherent, contained, and hopeful.

Excavating the Past: Pre-Intensive Assessments

Your client's intensive experience is kind of like those fixer-upper shows on home improvement networks.

When you first meet your clients, they know their house is in disarray, but they feel kind of lost. They're at their wit's end with what to do—they know this place could be beautiful, but somewhere along the way, life got messy, and they've lost direction.

You walk around the house with them, calling out the potential in a couple of rooms, identifying their hopes and dreams, and maybe pointing out things they might not have even noticed since they've been living in this situation for so long.

This stage is your pre-intensive process. It invites your client to take ownership of the intensive experience. Together with your professional guidance, they are able to define with you what it is they want to change (these are their goals) and what it is they want to achieve (these are their desired outcomes).

Without this tour of the past and this collaborative assessment of where things currently stand, your client might feel offended about all of the things you think are wrong with the place. They're not *that* bad of a housekeeper! They *like* that wallpaper! If you skip this step and jump right into demolition (therapy), they might feel overwhelmed, misunderstood, or judged. And worse, you might miss something important the client cares a lot about.

On the other hand, if you pull out your proposed blueprint plus the ten-step guide that's going to make their life all better, they will probably feel like there's no point in spending three days with you. There's no surprise, no self-discovery, no revelatory experience that will root these new tools in their lived experience. They could have just downloaded a tip sheet with coping skills on it from the internet. The point is, don't give away all of your tools and tricks before the intensive has even started. Keep these things reserved so that you can give them the magic of this moment.

Day One: Demo Day

Okay, it's Day 1 of your intensive: demo day!

Remember that tour of the home and all of its flaws and necessary fixes beforehand? It's time to get out the sledgehammers and expose the foundation.

We are very intentional about beginning our intensives in the past. Excavation is hard work. Sometimes there are more rotten boards than we expected, and whew! That mold! We've got to do something about that.

We'll go into therapeutic techniques in another chapter to help your client explore their past effectively. Be ready for surprises. The past is a wild place.

At the end of Day 1, your client might feel defeated. This is the part in the fixer-upper show where the homeowner stands in the middle of the rubble with her hands on her hips, shaking her head at the mess. How will we ever get out of this?

As your client's trusted guide, you'll want to end the day with material that is going to help them care for their hearts and minds. You might have some self-care tools and resources to offer them while they are apart from you. You might want them to journal about their experience. You may have some homework they need to do to prepare for what's next.

Demo day, or rather, the first day of our intensives, is often the hardest day for our clients. Deep truths and some unfamiliar territory is covered. The best thing for our clients at the end of Day 1 is to remind them of their goals, show them the next steps to come tomorrow, and reassure them they are on their way to recovery and healing. And then send them home to rest!

Renovating the Present: Day Two

By the second day, the demolition is complete. Day 1 is over and the house is down to the rafters and floorboards. It doesn't look like much, but boy, it turns out this house has good bones.

It's time to get to work with the rebuild. This is Renovation Day—the time to start rebuilding.

During the second day of an intensive, a lot of therapeutic work is done to connect the wounds and rubble of the past to the present circumstances that brought your clients into your office in the first place.

That mold over in the corner that's been making you sick all this time? It's from the leaky pipes we found yesterday, remember? It wasn't enough to clean up the mold. We had to get to the source of the problem. So what are we going to do to fix the pipe?

That's the idea here. An effective Day 2 helps clients integrate the work they did to explore their past situations the previous day with the current circumstances. You can expect a lot of wide-eyed, *aha* moments on Day 2 as you guide your client through various therapeutic practices and psychoeducation.

The work on Day 2 is active and engaging. Clients are no longer just looking back; they are learning to understand how the past continues to exert influence today. Together, we begin crafting strategies for interrupting harmful patterns, building healthier coping mechanisms, and strengthening emotional resilience.

This stage often brings a noticeable shift in energy. By the end of Day 2, the renovation is just about complete. The design team has been hard at work hanging drywall. The floor plan makes so much more sense now. There's a door where there should've been a door all along. The closet, oh wow, you guys, there's an amazing walk-in closet and there aren't *any more ghosts in it*.

Clients who ended Day 1 feeling burdened or overwhelmed frequently leave Day 2 with a new glimmer of hope. They begin to see that change is not only possible—it is already happening. The emotional load feels lighter, and the vision for a different future grows sharper.

It's been another long day of rebuilding, but tomorrow, you get to send your client out with some exciting final surprises that will lift them up and empower them for the future.

Preparing for the Future: Day Three

Overnight, the design team has been putting the finishing touches on the renovation. They've incorporated a special wall feature, with some photographs of times when life was good. They remembered the client's goal—open floor plan, brighter and more natural light, a master suite—and wow, architect, you've delivered. Now it's time to show off how they're going to live in this house.

Day 3 of the intensive is kind of like the big reveal. The hard work of excavation and renovation has been done, and now it is time to show the client what they have built—and what they can continue to build.

Day 3 is devoted to future focus. Having uncovered the sources of old pain and established new ways of relating to the present, the client is now ready to look ahead. Together, we lay down a path toward continued growth, outlining the practices, supports, and habits that will help maintain the progress made during the intensive.

Future planning on Day 3 includes identifying healthy coping strategies, building relapse prevention plans if needed, and establishing aftercare resources. We often discuss the importance of self-care rhythms, relational boundaries, community support, and therapeutic follow-up. By anchoring the client's insights into practical action steps, we help them leave the intensive feeling empowered and prepared—not abandoned or overwhelmed.

Throughout this final day, it is vital to celebrate progress. Clients need to hear that their efforts have mattered, that the shifts they have experienced are real and meaningful. They need to believe, not just intellectually but viscerally, that their lives can be different. Day 3 is about leaving them with a tangible sense of accomplishment and the tools to continue the work beyond our time together.

The Final Credits: Aftercare

There's always that moment at the end of fixer-upper shows where the camera crew comes back once the family has moved back into their renovated home. It shows Dad cooking, the kids playing in their rec room, Mom folding laundry and putting her clothes away in her great, new closet. Everything seems like it's on the right track now.

Your work isn't done when the intensive ends. Aftercare appointments with your clients are opportunities to check in with your client after their intensive experience to make sure they are making progress on their goals. Aftercare doesn't leave your client hanging, which is important when they're pleased with their intensive but essential when the experience is especially hard. You don't want your client to feel abandoned after their experience.

In my practice that focuses on trauma and addiction, aftercare has become an essential ingredient for my clients to maintain sobriety, healing, and accountability. Your clients might have a different focus than mine, but even so, some kind of aftercare experience is an essential part of your program, so that your clients can be as healthy and whole as they can be.

The Power of Environment and Experience

While the structure of the intensive provides the journey, the environment provides the setting—and it matters more than you might think.

Every element of your physical space shapes the client's experience: the lighting, the seating arrangement, the colors on the walls, even the scent in the air. A well-designed environment communicates safety, calm, and care before a single word is spoken.

Similarly, the emotional environment—the tone you set, the way you pace sessions, the balance between intensity and reflection—can make the difference between a client who feels overwhelmed and a client who feels deeply held. Thoughtful transitions between topics, carefully timed breaks, and the integration of experiential activities like journaling, art, or somatic practices all help clients engage more fully with the work.

In an intensive, we are asking clients to undertake brave and often painful emotional journeys. The least we can do is create a space that nurtures their courage.

Building Experiences, Not Just Sessions

In designing your intensive, remember that you are building an experience, not merely stringing together sessions. The journey must feel coherent, progressive, and meaningful. Clients should sense that each day builds naturally on the one before, leading them deeper into understanding and forward into action.

While the Past-Present-Future framework offers one effective model, it is not the only one. What matters most is that your structure makes emotional and psychological sense—that it allows your client to experience a complete arc of discovery, integration, and empowerment.

When intensives are designed with this level of intentionality, they become transformative experiences. They do not just offer insight; they create momentum. They do not just help clients understand their stories; they help them change their lives.

What will you fill this powerful structure and environment with to help your clients make that transformation? That's what we'll turn to next.

CHAPTER 11

Therapeutic Tools and Modalities

Integrative approaches in intensive therapy refer to the incorporation of multiple therapeutic modalities or techniques into a cohesive treatment plan tailored to suit your client's needs.

In an intensive, your clients are trusting you to provide the best treatment possible, not just what is typical. It's essential as practitioners we educate our clients on the various levels of care to ensure they can make the best and most informed decisions regarding treatment.

Compared to traditional therapeutic approaches, intensives are the perfect space for taking an integrative approach to therapy. Usually, traditional therapy settings adhere to limited theoretical orientations and modalities. Traditional therapy can have structural constraints, inadequate resources, insurance conflicts, quality control issues, or client expectations that limit the therapist's ability to incorporate multiple therapeutic techniques effectively.

But with a standard intensive, and three full days available to you, there is ample time, space, and freedom to design an intensive that builds upon your breadth of expertise and therapeutic practices!

Customization and Flexibility: Integrative therapy allows you to tailor treatment plans to the specific needs, preferences, and goals of each client.

Comprehensive Treatment: An integrative approach draws from different theoretical orientations and evidence-based practices, addressing various aspects of an individual's mental health. This comprehensive approach can target emotional, cognitive, behavioral, and interpersonal issues simultaneously, leading to more effective and holistic treatment outcomes.

Adaptability to Complex Cases: Intensive therapy often involves clients with complex and multifaceted issues, such as trauma, addiction, or mental and personality disorders. TIM's integrative approach allows therapists to combine interventions from different modalities to address these complexities comprehensively.

Enhanced Therapeutic Alliance: By offering a diverse range of therapeutic techniques, integrative therapy enables therapists to build stronger therapeutic alliances more quickly with clients. When clients feel that their unique needs are understood and addressed through a personalized approach, they are more likely to engage actively in the therapeutic process.

Maximization of Resources: Integrative therapy maximizes the resources available to therapists by incorporating techniques from various theoretical orientations and evidence-based practices. This allows therapists to draw upon a broader range of tools and interventions, optimizing treatment outcomes without being limited by the constraints of a single approach.

Increased Effectiveness: Research suggests that integrative approaches can be as effective as or even more effective than single-modality therapies for certain conditions. By integrating complementary techniques, therapists can capitalize on the strengths of each approach while mitigating their limitations, thereby enhancing overall effectiveness.

Empowerment and Self-Efficacy: Integrative therapy often includes psychoeducation and skill-building components, empowering clients to develop coping strategies and problem-solving skills that they can apply beyond the therapy sessions. This focus on building self-efficacy fosters greater autonomy and resilience in clients, contributing to long-term positive outcomes.

You might be wondering whether you need to have multiple specialties in order to offer an intensive. It's certainly not a requirement for intensive therapy, but you might consider exploring specializations as you develop your intensive-based practice.

While the toolbox of modalities can be fun to experiment with, you also want to be selective about how you combine different training techniques. Just because you have a particular tool in your toolbox doesn't mean you need to use it. It's also essential you have adequate training and experience in the tools you select to remain ethically sound.

There's danger in offering a particular tool just for the sake of doing something different. Stan Tatkin, author of *What Every Therapist Ought to Know*, says, "You can use all these tools, but you have to use them in accordance with your narrative, otherwise people get confused... Here we're using things in service of our therapeutic narrative." Tatkin also cautions, the use of variation is not the same as eclecticism and believes therapists ought to know the difference. He states, "A lot of this has to do with the mental organization of the therapist, one that's coherent, and fully organized, and focused."[16]

Remember, you're crafting a therapeutic experience for your client. You don't want to confuse them with many different techniques that lack some kind of cohesive story your client can't follow. Return to that therapeutic narrative and make sure that the techniques and modalities you choose serve the story your client is traveling through.

Let's take a look at five common therapeutic approaches and the ones I most commonly use in my intensive sessions.

Cognitive-Behavioral Therapy (CBT)

CBT targets the relationship between thoughts, feelings, and behaviors. It aims to identify and change negative thought patterns and maladaptive behaviors. CBT uses cognitive restructuring, behavioral experiments, exposure therapy, and relaxation techniques. It is effective for treating anxiety disorders, depression, PTSD, phobias, and various other mental health issues.

Experiential Therapy

Experiential therapy emphasizes the importance of emotional experiences in therapy. It encourages clients to explore and express emotions rather than solely focusing on cognition. Experiential therapy uses role-playing, guided imagery, expressive arts, and somatic experiencing. It is useful for addressing unresolved trauma, relationship issues, emotional regulation difficulties, and personal growth.

---

16 *Stan Tatkin, What Every Therapist Ought to Know: Attachment, Arousal Regulation, and Clinical Techniques in Couple Therapy (Sounds True, 2021).*

Interpersonal Neurobiology (IPNB)

IPNB integrates principles from neuroscience, psychology, and interpersonal relationships to understand how the brain and relationships shape each other. It emphasizes the importance of social connections in mental health. IPNB uses mindfulness practices, attuned communication, and fostering secure attachments. It is applied in therapy to enhance emotional regulation, empathy, and relational skills, particularly in the context of trauma recovery and interpersonal difficulties.

Solution-Focused Brief Therapy (SFBT)

SFBT emphasizes identifying and amplifying the client's strengths and resources to generate solutions. It focuses on setting clear, achievable goals and implementing small changes to create positive outcomes. SFBT uses miracle questions, scaling questions, exception finding, and solution-building conversations. SFBT is particularly suited for short-term therapy, crisis intervention, and situations where clients are motivated to make changes but may not want to delve deeply into past issues.

Trauma-Informed Therapy

Trauma-informed therapy recognizes the widespread impact of trauma on individuals and emphasizes creating a safe and empowering therapeutic environment. It focuses on understanding trauma symptoms and fostering resilience. Trauma-informed therapy utilizes trauma-focused cognitive-behavioral therapy (TF-CBT), Eye Movement Desensitization and Reprocessing (EMDR), somatic experiencing, and grounding techniques. Trauma-informed therapy is essential for working with individuals who have experienced trauma, including PTSD, childhood abuse, and other adverse experiences. It aims to promote healing, recovery, and empowerment while minimizing re-traumatization.

Every approach has specific benefits to offer clients. Some fit practitioners based on your preferences or giftedness, and some will suit your client better, depending on their needs. If you are versed in a variety of different approaches, you will have more options and opportunities to vary and customize the intensive experience for your client.

The Difference between Approaches and Modalities

It might help here to differentiate between therapeutic approaches and therapeutic modalities. **Counseling approaches** emphasize broad theoretical frameworks whereas **counseling modalities** offer specific protocols and certifications. Let's look a little closer at the two:

Counseling Approaches: Counseling approaches focus on overarching theories and principles that guide the therapeutic process. They provide a framework for understanding human behavior, emotions, and relationships but allow flexibility in implementing techniques based on individual client needs.

Some examples of counseling approaches include those we've already taken a look at as well as others, like Psychodynamic Therapy, Humanistic/ Person-Centered Therapy, and Existential Therapy.

Some of the distinctive characteristics of counseling approaches are:

- *How flexible they are.* Therapists are able to adapt interventions based on the unique needs and goals of each client.
- *Their emphasis on relationship.* The therapeutic alliance and rapport between therapist and client play a crucial role in the effectiveness of the approach.
- *Their broad application.* These approaches can be applied to a wide range of mental health issues and populations.
- *Their focus on understanding.* With these approaches, therapists prioritize understanding the underlying factors contributing to the client's difficulties.

Counseling Modalities: On the other hand, modalities offer structured, manualized protocols with specific techniques and interventions. Therapists must undergo specialized training and certification to deliver these interventions effectively.

Some examples of modalities include Dialectical Behavior Therapy (DBT), Eye Movement Desensitization and Reprocessing (EMDR), Trauma-Focused Cognitive-Behavioral Therapy (TF-CBT), and Emotionally Focused Therapy (EFT).

Counseling modalities are:

- *Structured:* These interventions are standardized and follow specific protocols outlined in training manuals or guidelines.
- *Targeted:* Each modality typically addresses specific issues or populations, such as trauma, addiction, or couples therapy.
- *Require Certification:* Therapists undergo specialized training and certification to ensure competence in delivering the modality.
- *Evidence-Based:* Many of these modalities have a substantial body of research supporting their effectiveness for particular issues.

To sum up the difference between approaches and modalities, think of it this way: Broad theoretical approaches offer flexibility in adapting interventions to individual client needs, while specific modalities provide structured protocols for targeted issues.

Therapists specializing in specific modalities typically obtain certification through formal training programs, whereas those utilizing broad approaches may have general training in counseling or psychotherapy.

While both types of approaches can address various mental health concerns, modalities with specific protocols often have a more defined scope of application based on their focus area (e.g., trauma, addiction, relationship issues).

Creating Your Top Tools Toolkit

While you're thinking about the various kinds of approaches and modalities available for intensives, take some time to brainstorm a list of your favorite interventions. I like to keep this document open on my laptop or tablet during an intensive so that I can reference it at any time. That document has content that is applicable to both individuals and couples.

You can also keep binders of extra copies of handouts on the bookshelf in your office. I organize mine by topic: couples, family of origin, trauma, and addiction. For each binder, there are sections for more specific topics, like anger, communication, and forgiveness. I keep a master copy in a page protector and then try to keep about five copies available to give away. Of course, you might prefer keeping digital files over hard copies. If that's the case, just have an office printer handy to run off a copy quickly for your client.

The key is keeping your material organized and easy to access for those moments during a session when your client says something that makes you want to shift to a different approach.

Personally, I always have my laptop up in session to take notes as well as access content on the fly. You can create a Google Drive folder for top tools and interventions and make it a favorite folder. You might also want to have a tablet available for your clients so they can easily access videos, assessments, and specific Google Drive folders without needing to print. They can even screenshot and AirDrop handouts to their phone if they want.

Now that we've looked at a handful of approaches and modalities available for your intensives, let's talk through how you can leverage experiential and expressive therapies in The Intensive Method.

CHAPTER 12

Experiential and Expressive Therapy Options

There are some feelings and emotions our clients just can't put into words.

Imagine your client walking slowly to a shelf you have in your office, lined with miniature figures—animals, people, trees, doors, fences, fire, and keys. She studies them for a moment, then selects a handful and begins arranging them in a sand tray. She puts a lone figure in the center, surrounded by a jagged line of soldiers. In the corner, she sets up a tiny house, hidden behind a wall. As she moves the pieces, her breathing changes. Her eyes begin to fill, though she hasn't spoken a word. You ask her what she sees, and slowly, a story emerges. It isn't just a memory but a felt sense of isolation, fear, and longing. As the client arranges the miniatures in the tray, it becomes a landscape of her inner world, one she can now observe, reshape, and eventually, reclaim.

Experiential and expressive therapies like this can help your clients engage in a different way, allowing for profound exploration and processing of thoughts, feelings, and experiences. These therapies move the client out of cognitive processing into a multifaceted experience. Being actively engaged in the therapeutic process in this way can foster a sense of agency and empowerment. As in the above case, these therapies can be particularly beneficial for clients who have a difficult time articulating their feelings or experiences verbally.

Being able to engage other senses and other areas of the brain when processing difficult subject matter can make a world of difference for your clients, and the intensive space is an ideal environment for just that.

Many practitioners will have stuffed animals, puppets, toys, Lego, etc. that they can allow clients to manipulate in session as a form of expression. Using right brain techniques like writing or drawing in color or with the non-dominant hand can be powerful for new insights. Sometimes just movement makes a big difference. I have a client who likes to pace in my office. Some like to walk and talk, even in a circle, while others prefer the old-school Freudian method of lying down on the couch and spreading out.

Even just taking off their shoes, having a cozy blanket or teddy bear, and offering them a warm cup of coffee can be nice approaches when doing trauma-based work, so clients can be as comfortable as possible.

Let's take a look at several different examples of possible experiential therapies and expressive therapies that you might employ during your intensives along with examples of how these sessions might unfold.

Experiential Therapy: Gestalt Therapy

Gestalt therapy focuses on the present moment experience and emphasizes awareness of thoughts, emotions, and behaviors. Techniques such as role-playing, empty chair work, and guided imagery are commonly used.

Imagine you're midway through a 3-day intensive with a client who has carried decades of unspoken grief and resentment toward his older brother. He's insightful, articulate, even emotionally aware—but there's a wall he can't seem to break through. So, on the second afternoon, you set out a chair across from him and say, "Let's invite your brother into the room."

He hesitates. You can see the resistance in his eyes. But you gently guide him: *What does he look like? What's his posture? What's the expression on his face as he listens to you?* Slowly, your client begins to speak. At first, it's guarded—then it becomes raw. Anger gives way to sorrow. Defensiveness turns to longing. Eventually, you invite him to sit in the other chair and respond as his brother. At first, he shakes his head—but then he tries, and something breaks open. It isn't a resolution, necessarily, but your client has made a shift. He's softened and come to a deeper understanding of the story he's been living inside.

It's your job as the therapist to guide your client in expressing their feelings and engaging in a dialogue with the imaginary presence, helping them explore what they were unable to access simply by talking it out.

Experiential Therapy: Psychodrama

Psychodrama involves role-playing scenarios or conflicts from the client's life. In an intensive therapy session, a therapist might facilitate a psychodrama where the client reenacts a significant event or relationship dynamic. Other group members can participate as supporting characters, and the therapist guides the client in exploring different perspectives and resolutions.

Imagine your client is a woman in her early forties, participating in a weekend intensive group. She's shared parts of her story, rooted in a childhood marked by emotional neglect and the impossible task of trying to keep peace in a chaotic home. She keeps returning to one story in particular: the night she made dinner for her parents to stop them from fighting. You can tell there's more behind it, so you invite her into a psychodrama.

With the support of the group, she casts others to play her mother, her father, and her nine-year-old self. She takes her place offstage at first, watching. The scene begins. Her child-self anxiously sets the table, placing a bowl of spaghetti just so, hoping that food could silence the storm. As the reenactment unfolds, tears stream down her face.

Then, gently, you invite her to step into the role of the child. She hesitates and then walks forward. Her voice trembles as she repeats the words she once said. When she switches roles to embody her mother, something shifts. She finally says the words she's longed to hear, "This wasn't yours to fix."

The moment is tender and brave—and something inside her begins to unfreeze.

When your client is given the opportunity to look at their experiences from different perspectives in a psychodrama, they often gain new insights, emotional clarity, and a sense of empowerment that can be difficult to access through words alone.

Let's shift now, from these two examples of experiential therapies, to a few examples of expressive therapies.

Expressive Therapy: Art Therapy

Art therapy utilizes various art forms (such as painting, drawing, sculpture, etc.) as a means of expression and exploration. In an intensive therapy session, a therapist might incorporate art therapy by providing materials for clients to create visual representations of their emotions, inner conflicts, or experiences. The therapist then facilitates a discussion around the artwork, helping the client gain insights and process their feelings.

Imagine a client, let's call him Mark, sitting in your office. He's silent and tense, poised on the edge of the couch. It's been a rough intensive so far; Mark hasn't been able to open up much. He's been on guard all morning. You let him know that you're going to try something different this afternoon, pointing to the corner of the room where you've prepared a large canvas and several jars of paint during your lunch break.

You tell Mark, "You don't have to explain how you feel right now. Just show me what your anger feels like."

Mark reluctantly picks up a brush, making small and tentative strokes across the canvas at first. Soon, however, his movements start to grow more intense. He slashes broad swaths of red and black across the white space. As he moves the brush, he isn't just painting; he's remembering, feeling, and releasing. Grief, betrayal, and a lifetime of bottled-up resentment pour out of him in color and motion. When he finally steps back from the canvas, he looks exhausted, but lighter. His tone of voice is different when he begins to speak, able to articulate his thoughts for the first time in days without defensiveness or edginess.

Moments like these remind us that healing doesn't always begin with words. It often begins with expression. In intensive therapy, art can become a bridge between what a client feels and what they're able to say, opening up new pathways for insight, integration, and emotional release.

Expressive Therapy: Music Therapy

Music therapy works the same way as art therapy, only in this case, we're employing a different medium for creating. Music therapy involves the use of music and sound to address emotional, cognitive, and social needs. You might integrate music therapy by inviting clients to engage in activities such as songwriting, improvisation, or listening to specific pieces of music that resonate with their experiences. From there, you can facilitate discussions about the emotions and memories evoked by the music.

Imagine your client is a teenage girl named Maya, guarded and quiet through most of your intensive sessions. When asked how she feels, she usually says, "I don't know" or offers a small shrug. On the second afternoon, you ask if she'd be willing to share a song that feels like her.

She hesitates, then pulls out her phone and plays a track—slow, haunting, with a steady beat and lyrics about feeling invisible. You both listen in silence. When the song ends, you ask gently, "What part of that song feels most true to you?"

She pauses, then points to a lyric: *"I scream but no one hears me."*

For the first time all day, she begins to speak—not about the song exactly, but about what it feels like to keep everything inside. She talks about how music sometimes says what she can't. You follow her lead, and soon, a conversation begins to unfold—emerging from melody, memory, and meaning.

Music creates a space where clients can project, connect, and reflect, sometimes revealing more in a single lyric than an entire hour of questions ever could.

The Sky's the Limit

There are of course more options available beyond these four. What might suit your clientele? What suits your style? These are all additional ways you can differentiate yourself from other practitioners. You might also think about whether there are local businesses that offer the kinds of activities described above or listed below for potential partnerships. Some of these are out-of-the-box ideas, but since you're exploring intensives, I'm guessing you're probably an out-of-the-box practitioner! As long as you are ethical and follow appropriate guidelines to protect yourself and your clients, don't be afraid to get creative!

You might take a moment now to jot down any ideas that stand out to you or ones you might want to investigate further. Here are a few ideas to help you get started:

Expressive Therapies:	Experiential Therapies:
• Art Therapy • Music Therapy • Dance/Movement Therapy • Drama Therapy • Poetry Therapy • Play Therapy (including sandplay therapy and therapeutic play) • Writing Therapy (including journaling and narrative therapy) • Phototherapy • Digital Art Therapy • Expressive Arts Therapy (integrating multiple art forms)	• Gestalt Therapy • Psychodrama • Somatic Experiencing • Mindfulness-Based Stress Reduction (MBSR) • EMDR (Eye Movement Desensitization and Reprocessing) • Equine-Assisted Therapy • Adventure Therapy • Wilderness Therapy • Play Therapy (in an experiential context) • Body Psychotherapy (including Hakomi Therapy and Bioenergetic Analysis)

Tips for Incorporating Expressive and Experiential Therapy

When you're ready to introduce a new experiential or expressive therapy to your client, you can make it the best experience by following these steps:

Assessment and Tailoring: Rely on the pre-intensive assessments, preferences, and therapeutic goals you collect from your client prior to the intensive to help you tailor their experience.

Self-Care: At the beginning of every session, do a feelings check with your client to be present and aware of their needs. As with all therapeutic approaches and modalities, both you and your clients need to prioritize self-care and emotional resilience.

Flexibility and Adaptability: Start experiential work slowly, with a light version on the first day. If they respond well and would like to do more, you have Days 2 and 3 to add more. Different clients may respond differently to various interventions, so you should be prepared to modify approaches as needed to meet individual needs.

Establishing Safety: When you introduce new activities, it will help your client feel comfortable if they have adequate training, clear guidelines, and established boundaries. As your clients explore sensitive and challenging material, you will want to be prepared to provide emotional support.

Expressive and experiential therapies offer clients powerful, nonverbal ways to access and process their inner world. Whether through art, movement, drama, or music, these approaches create space for healing where words fall short, inviting clients to feel, reflect, and reimagine their stories. In the context of an intensive, they can serve as emotional catalysts, unlocking deeper layers of insight and movement.

As we turn our attention to the next chapter, we'll explore how these same principles—presence, creativity, and embodiment—can support clients in the midst of trauma and crisis, when regulation is fragile and the therapeutic container must hold even more.

CHAPTER 13

Addressing Trauma and Crisis

Some people may be drawn to intensives because they need a higher level of care, and being able to offer a higher level of care with intensive outpatient options is certainly helpful. However, you'll want to pay close attention during your screening process to make sure that you have the appropriate level of experience or expertise to address the needs of your potential clients. We'll go over the screening process for intensives in detail in the next chapter.

Once you begin responding to client applications and start your screening process, there will likely be cases that are beyond your scope of practice, are outside of your specialization, or may require additional care or specialized service than you are able to offer. If that's the case, having a good referral list will help make sure that, even if you aren't able to help a particular client, you won't leave them hanging. Make sure that your referral list includes resources for inpatient or other extended IOP programs.

Dealing with Complex Trauma and Crisis Situations in Intensives

Beyond your screening process, it's important to have a plan for managing trauma and crisis during your intensives. As I've mentioned before, intensive therapy is intense. It's important for you to enter into your intensive offerings with clarity of mind and a clear plan for navigating complex trauma and crisis situations. You need to be just as prepared to deal with these scenarios in an intensive setting as you would be in regular therapy.

Let's imagine that it's late afternoon on the second day of a 3-day intensive. Your client, Leah, has been edging closer to a painful memory involving childhood abuse. During a somatic exercise, something cracks open. She freezes, then begins to sob uncontrollably. Her breathing becomes rapid, and she curls into herself, trembling. You recognize the signs of dissociation and escalating distress, but you're caught off guard. You fumble for your notes, trying to recall what grounding techniques you'd planned to use. Your voice is tight as you ask, "What are you feeling right now?"

Leah doesn't respond. You try again, this time a little louder, "Do you want to talk about what's happening?" She flinches. The silence grows heavy. Instead of pausing to assess her safety or regulate the space, you press forward, hoping to salvage the momentum: "We were just starting to get somewhere—can you stay with this?" At that moment, Leah bolts upright and says, "I need to leave." She grabs her bag, rushes out, and doesn't return your calls that evening.

What went wrong? This situation escalated because **key principles for navigating the crisis** were missed. The therapist's own discomfort prevented them from staying **calm and grounded**. There was no clear **safety assessment** or response to signs of dissociation. **Active listening** and **grounding techniques** were not employed, and the therapist unknowingly **crossed a boundary** by urging the client to "stay with it" rather than prioritizing regulation and choice. In failing to maintain **rapport and trust**, the therapist inadvertently confirmed the client's worst fear: that therapy is not a safe place when things fall apart.

Navigating a crisis situation during an intensive therapy session requires practitioners to be well-prepared, calm, and adaptable. Let's look a little closer at some tips to help you navigate such situations effectively.

Remain Calm and Grounded: It's essential to stay calm and composed during a crisis. Your demeanor can help reassure the client and maintain a sense of safety in the therapeutic environment.

Assess for Safety: Prioritize assessing the immediate safety of the client and others involved in the situation. Determine if there are any immediate risks of harm and take appropriate action to address them.

Establish Rapport and Trust: If the crisis involves heightened emotions or distress, focus on building rapport and trust with the client. Validate their feelings and reassure them that you're there to support them through the crisis.

Utilize Grounding Techniques: Grounding techniques can help clients stay present and connected during intense emotional experiences. Encourage the client to focus on their breath, use sensory grounding techniques, or engage in other calming activities.

Maintain Boundaries: While it's important to provide support and empathy, practitioners should also maintain professional boundaries during a crisis. Clearly communicate your role and limitations, and avoid overstepping boundaries or taking on responsibilities beyond your scope of practice.

Collaborative Problem-Solving: Involve the client in problem-solving and decision-making whenever possible. Empower them to take an active role in managing the crisis and identifying coping strategies that work for them.

Use Active Listening: Practice active listening skills to fully understand the client's perspective and experiences. Reflect back their feelings and concerns to demonstrate empathy and validation.

Utilize Crisis Intervention Techniques: Draw on your training in crisis intervention techniques to de-escalate the situation and help the client regain a sense of control. This may involve using calming language, providing reassurance, and exploring coping strategies together.

Consultation and Collaboration: If the crisis situation exceeds your expertise or resources, don't hesitate to seek consultation or collaborate with other mental health professionals or emergency services. Prioritize the client's safety and well-being above all else.

Follow-Up and Support: After the crisis has been managed, ensure ongoing support and follow-up with the client as needed. Offer resources, referrals, or additional sessions to help them process the experience and develop long-term coping strategies. I often give my clients my cell phone number (or you can set up a Google phone number that keeps your number private), and if there are needs that arise, even in the evening of an intensive, I have them reach out to me. I often check-in with them anyway, especially if we've had an extremely difficult day.

Equipped with these strategies, let's imagine the same moment again with Leah and how it could have gone differently:

Leah begins to cry, her breath quickens, and she curls up, clearly overwhelmed.

You pause and take a breath yourself. Then, gently and quietly, you say, "You're safe here. I'm right here with you. Let's slow everything down." You lower your own voice and posture. You ask softly, "Can you tell me one thing you can feel right now?" You help her focus on the texture of the blanket she's holding, the coolness of the floor under her feet. You **assess for safety**, noting her dissociation cues, but see she's still responsive. "You're not alone. I'm here," you repeat as she begins to settle.

Once Leah stabilizes, you don't push forward. Instead, you **validate her courage** and invite her to rest. "What you just touched is huge. You don't have to do any more today. We'll take care of you." You check in later that evening with a quick text: "Just wanted you to know I'm thinking of you. You did really hard work today. Let me know if you need anything."

She replies, "Thank you. I'm okay. I really appreciate that."

The Difference That Makes the Difference: When a therapist remains calm, grounded, and attuned, even moments of crisis can become turning points for healing rather than retraumatization. By assessing safety, employing grounding strategies, maintaining boundaries, and collaborating with the client, you create a container strong enough to hold their pain—and safe enough to return to.

You're the Guide

No matter what your client is dealing with, they don't expect you to be a miracle worker. They will trust your ability to help them navigate their next steps, even if that is having to make a report, recommend inpatient or psych services, or, worst-case scenario, contact the police.

Remember, you can always pause, take a break, or utilize your next break as an opportunity to contact a supervisor or trusted consultant to seek guidance if you are unsure what to do next. This is another great benefit of The Intensive Method; you will have ample time to pivot treatment if it is warranted.

Creating a Trauma-Sensitive Environment

There's a lot more to be said about trauma-informed care and whole certification programs available for practitioners. In my practice (Hope & Freedom) we have very intentional tools we give to all Certified Hope & Freedom Practitioners that provide targeted support for the niche clientele we serve. You may want to invest more time and effort into developing this particular area of expertise for your practice, or seek certifications like we offer through the Hope & Freedom Institute.

In the meantime, here are some tips to help you establish a trauma-sensitive environment for your clients:

Create a Safe Environment: Establishing a safe and supportive environment is paramount in trauma-sensitive therapy. Ensure that the therapy space feels comfortable and secure, and communicate clearly about confidentiality and boundaries.

Empower Client Autonomy: Respect the client's autonomy and empower them to make decisions about their therapy. Offer choices whenever possible and involve them in treatment planning and goal-setting.

Practice Cultural Sensitivity: Be mindful of cultural differences and how they may impact the therapeutic process. Respect and honor the client's cultural background, beliefs, and values, and consider how these factors may influence their experiences of trauma and healing.

Normalize Responses to Trauma: Validate the client's emotional reactions and normalize common responses to trauma, such as hypervigilance, dissociation, or emotional numbing. Help them understand that these responses are adaptive survival mechanisms.

Use Trauma-Informed Language: Be mindful of the language you use and its potential impact on trauma survivors. Avoid using language that blames or shames the client, and instead use validating and empowering language that fosters a sense of safety and trust.

Practice Grounding Techniques: Teach clients grounding techniques to help them stay present and regulated during therapy sessions. This may include deep breathing exercises, mindfulness practices, or sensory grounding techniques.

Encourage Self-Care: Emphasize the importance of self-care and help clients develop self-soothing strategies to manage distress outside of therapy sessions. Encourage healthy coping mechanisms such as exercise, creative expression, and spending time in nature.

Monitor for Triggers: Be vigilant for potential triggers and help clients identify and manage them effectively. Create a plan for coping with triggers as they arise during therapy sessions, and ensure that the client feels safe and supported throughout the process.

Provide Psychoeducation: Offer psychoeducation about trauma and its effects on the body and mind. Help clients understand the neurobiology of trauma and how it can impact their thoughts, emotions, and behaviors.

At this point, we've looked closely at the core service of intensives, from what you might cover during your intensive to how you might structure your intensive. You've also spent some time considering who your target audience is and how you might reach them. With these core components gaining some traction in your mind, it's now time for us to turn to how you can best prepare yourself *and* your clients for a successful intensive experience.

PART 4

Preparing You and Your Clients for Success

CHAPTER 14

Screening Clients for Fit

With a well defined intensive offering advertised clearly on your website and a key target audience in mind, you've already laid the groundwork for attracting the right kind of clients to your program. However, that doesn't mean everyone who applies to your intensive is going to be a shoe-in for this kind of experience. There are bound to be those who match your target audience characteristics who may not be a good fit for intensives.

It's important to keep this in mind when you build out your application and screening process. First, let's address general characteristics to look for in potential candidates. Then, we'll talk about some red flags to beware of in your screening and/or application process. Finally, we'll talk through how to set up a system for application and screening that will give you the structure and process to find and filter the best matches for your program.

Characteristics of Ideal Clients

So, who is a good fit for an intensive, and who isn't? Shouldn't anyone who needs your help be able to sign up for your intensive?

As we covered early on, intensives are not for everyone. You will have some specific qualifiers based on the type of intensive you're offering, but universally speaking, the best candidates for an intensive need to be **highly motivated** and possess a **high desire and commitment to change**. This is a substantial investment of both time and money. No one ought to come into an intensive with a high degree of reluctance or resistance to change. It's natural for people to enter the intensive experience with some anxiety about what the experience will be like, since most likely they've never engaged with an intensive before, but this reaction is different from reluctance or resistance to change. If someone has felt pressured into an intensive but does not currently possess the willingness to engage in a transformative process, the experience will not be transformative. Much depends upon your client's willingness to receive and respond to what you have to give during the intensive.

If you're offering couples intensives, both partners need to possess these same characteristics. A spouse cannot carry the weight of the couple if one partner is unwilling to commit to the effort involved with an intensive. That's why we require both partners to complete separate applications for intensives at Hope & Freedom.

Besides desire and motivation, ideal candidates should also demonstrate some **capacity for insight and self-reflection**. Individuals in an intensive need to be willing to explore their own behavior, take responsibility for their actions, and reflect honestly. This also requires some **openness to feedback**. The best candidates are open to receiving honest and sometimes challenging feedback in a supportive environment.

Finally, the ideal applicant might not know exactly what they need, but they do know that they're stuck, hurting, or seeking transformation in a specific area. They have **clear goals or pain points**, which often propels the work forward. Even if you've clearly articulated the purpose for your intensive and the pain points it addresses, some clients may not possess the same clarity about what it is they are experiencing, but those who *do* see their need for change tend to be more motivated to make change happen.

Red Flags and Contraindications

On the flip side, there are also several signals that indicate candidates may not be a good fit for an intensive. If the client has even low rates of comorbid issues that might require inpatient care, an intensive may not be a good fit for them as they may need a higher level of care. They also shouldn't have a history of psychosis or major mental disorders that could be contraindicated for several days of heavy emotional lifting.

I also would be reluctant to treat high-conflict couples who are impinging on divorce, have already engaged in divorce proceedings, or are currently separated physically... unless the intensive is specifically intended as an intervention for these types of couples and situations.

In addition, any candidates who have suicidal ideation or have planned or attempted suicide should be addressed and treated prior to any sort of acceptance for an intensive. Situations with domestic violence or abuse should also be addressed ahead of time. All situations that could involve self-harm or harm to someone else are very serious and are grounds for immediate attention.

There are some instances where clients may need a series of intensives to address multiple issues. For example, sometimes for complex couples I might treat one or both of them individually first, with an intensive geared toward trauma or family or origin, before I would conduct a couples intensive. For these types of scenarios, you want to be cognizant of possible triangulation and have a strong no-secrets policy in your program to protect you if you choose to work with couples. It's a strong benefit to work individual sessions during a couple's intensives; however, you also need to have good measures in place to protect yourself and the therapeutic alliance.

Be sure to consider establishing policies and procedures for your clients.[17] These issues may feel uncomfortable or intimidating; however, addressing them now is your best defense to avoid them later.

Your website should do some of the self-selecting work for you—your promotional materials should clearly articulate the basic structure, duration, and expectations of your intensive. You don't want to frighten people away, but you also don't want to oversell an intensive as an easy, breezy miracle cure for whatever ails them.

As Brené Brown says, clear is kind. Make sure your potential clients understand the nature of intensives before they go through your application process.

The Initial Application

A substantial amount of information needs to be collected before you ever speak with a potential client. Through the application, I can often screen out applicants who don't match the initial criteria, long before we ever advance to a screening call.

---

17 *A sample policy and procedures document is available through The Intensive Method online course or for download at theintensivemethod.com.*

My application at Hope & Freedom is a four-part form that requests detailed information about the client's personal life, occupation, relationship, family culture, type of therapy and intensive they're interested in, specifics about the condition for which they're seeking help, an inventory of past suicidal considerations, willingness to participate in certain aspects of recommended care, and an explanation of their commitment to recovery.[18]

This application is intentionally lengthy and detailed. If individuals or couples are unwilling to put in the work to provide this information upfront, then they are also unlikely to be strong candidates for intensive therapy. The information applicants provide will help you quickly rule out some candidates and determine which candidates ought to advance to a screening call.

All clients must submit an application to be considered, and as I mentioned earlier, if you're conducting couples therapy, both partners must submit separate applications in order to schedule a screening call with them. These applications should be kept confidential in their client file; however, these are completed prior to becoming a client, so the application form itself may or may not be protected under HIPAA, depending how you choose to create and have your forms submitted. You may elect to put a disclaimer on your form stating its nature if you prefer.

If you are considering a present client for an intensive, you might not require them to complete an application since you're already working with them. Regardless, you will still want to have some form of screening, even if it's during a session. Just make sure the client is okay with using their therapy time to process the potential for an intensive. If not, you may prefer to have them complete the application and allocate a separate time to process the intensive rather than using their therapy time for that purpose.

Scripts and Checklists for Screening Calls

After you've received your application, it's time to schedule a screening call... unless, of course, the applicant doesn't meet your initial criteria (we'll cover how to say "no" to those applicants later in this chapter).

---

18 *An intensive application template is available through The Intensive Method online course or for download at theintensivemethod.com.*

Your screening call serves as your first personal connection with your potential client. There are three main objectives to plan for on this call: covering the intensive details, asking your screening questions, and accepting or denying the client.

Intensive Details

It's important to go over the structural details of your intensive on this call, even if you have spelled this out in your marketing content and in a follow-up email to their application. People often need to hear material in lots of different ways before it sinks in, so it doesn't hurt to reiterate what they should expect from your intensive during your call. This portion of your call should only take about ten minutes or so; you want to leave the majority of the time available for potential clients to ask you their questions and for you to ask them your screening questions.

Screening Questions

In preparation for your call, draft a series of questions that will help you press into areas of your application that will help you get clarity on whether or not a person is motivated enough to participate in an intensive. You will want to ask scaling questions, like "On a scale of 1-10, how motivated are you to..." If you are conducting couples therapy, you will want both partners to answer that question, for themselves and about their partner.

You might also ask additional questions about the client's current symptoms, their history of mental health treatment, and any relevant medical or psychiatric issues. You may want to make sure you have some questions included to gauge a potential client's trauma history.[19] *Whatever you ask ought to be directed toward discerning if a client is a good candidate for your particular intensive.*

I recommend drafting a screening call script, screening questions, and a screening call checklist to use during your calls. This allows you to keep the conversation focused and direct, every time you conduct a new call.[20]

---

19 Trauma-related screening questions are available through The Intensive Method online course or for download at theintensivemethod.com.

20 A Screening Call Script Template is available through The Intensive Method online course or for download at theintensivemethod.com.

Client Acceptance/Denial

By the end of your screening call, it should be obvious to you whether or not this person or couple is a good candidate for an intensive with you, and you should tell them kindly and respectfully. Be sure to also let them know that, if you are unable to accept them, it isn't because you don't want to work with them; rather, you want them to get the treatment that is right for them.

Should you not accept them, they will probably be somewhat disappointed; after all, they are seeking your help! This is a prime opportunity to direct these individuals towards services you feel would be beneficial for them. You might suggest traditional outpatient therapy, group therapy, workshops, a psychiatrist or other medical professional, teletherapy, online counseling, community resources, and self-help resources. If you feel there's a chance the client could work with you at some point later down the road, provide the steps and expectations they would need to meet for reassessment.

If you have determined that the client makes a good candidate for an intensive, end your call by offering to schedule their intensive now, if they are ready to take that step, or if this doesn't work for your process, let them know that you'll be sending information to them after the call with the steps they need to take next. If they aren't ready to make a decision on your call, that's fine—some people need to take time to process whether they are ready to move forward. Just be sure to clearly state what they need to do next, and *follow-up* with every potential client after the call.

Some people ask if I charge for screening calls. Personally, I do not—I offer up to an hour and sometimes more for people that are considering an intensive, because it's a big investment for them, and it feels like the right thing for me to be able to give them that much time to make sure it's an informed decision. However, there's no hard and fast rule. If you feel that you need to charge for your time, then use your ethical guidelines and boundaries to define that and make it happen.

Follow-Up and Next Steps

Again, *all* applicants should receive some kind of follow-up communication after the call: If they've been denied, thank them for their time and remind them of the alternative care options you mentioned on the call.[21] This provides

---

21 *An Intensive Screening Call Denial Email template is available through The Intensive Method*

these potential candidates with a clear next step to pursue health, no matter what they came to you for.

The next step for those who have been accepted is to sign up for an intensive date and time. If they did not take this step at the end of your call, then extend the invitation again, perhaps including a date range or several options of next available opportunities, in your follow-up email. We give our clients a 30-day window from the time of their screening to schedule an intensive. If they don't respond during that time, they are required to reapply.

Once your potential clients have scheduled their intensive and paid whatever deposit you've required, it's time to prepare them for the intensive. In the next chapter, we'll cover what you need to build an effective assessment and intake process for intensives, including the systems and workflow that will help you make the process as simple and streamlined as possible for both you and your clients.

---

online course or for download at theintensivemethod.com.

CHAPTER 15

Assessment and Intake for Successful Intensives

Congratulations! You have accepted your first client for your intensive. Now it's time to begin collecting the information you need to have a successful experience. We covered ten steps to plan and prepare for an intensive with your client back in Chapter 4. That chapter was all about *what* to do. This chapter will cover *how* to do it. We want to help you establish the intake framework and flow that will work best for you and your client. This chapter will also go over some tools and processes you can use to make your system work best. Let's begin with your intake framework.

Establishing the Intake Framework

As we covered in Chapter 4, there is a lot of information you want to gather from your client after they've scheduled their intensive. The purpose of intake is both **clinical** and **relational**. The intake process provides you with insight into your client's core issues, presenting symptoms, and treatment history. It allows you to tailor the structure, pacing, and interventions of the intensives. After the screening call, it helps you continue to set expectations with your client about what to expect at the intensive.

From the client's perspective, completing the intake process fosters commitment and engagement, encouraging buy-in as they reflect on their goals, pain points, and other assessment questions. It also reduces your client's anxiety by providing them with structure and education about what they'll encounter during the intensive. A structured, clear intake process signals to your client that you are a professional—organized, prepared, and trustworthy—all of which will help the client feel safe as they enter into an environment that will likely demand their vulnerability.

Whatever you choose to collect from your client ought to inform how you shape the intensive experience. We'll go over what you can do to customize your client's treatment plan based on the results of assessments and intake in the next chapter.

Designing Your Intake Process

Clearly, the intake process is an important part of onboarding your clients for the intensive. As you design your intake flow, here are some factors to consider:

Clear Protocols: Begin developing clear protocols and guidelines for scheduling, intake, and preparation for 3-day intensives. What are your rules for scheduling? Perhaps you only want to schedule intensives from Thursday to Saturday. What is your cancellation policy? What forms and assessments need to be completed before a client can come to the intensive? Clear guidelines for onboarding will ensure that the process is run the same every time a new client begins working with you.

Comprehensive and Standardized Intake Forms: Evaluate all of the information you need to collect from your client prior to the intensive, and then create forms that gather all of that information. These forms should include mental health history, current symptoms, treatment goals, and any specific concerns that need to be addressed.

Send your clients as many assessments as you need to get a clear picture of where they are coming from before they arrive. These are optional and might be available from your EHR software if you utilize one, or you can customize your assessments.[22]

Pre-Intensive Preparation Sessions: Conduct a pre-intensive preparation discussion, either over the phone or in-session with current clients to discuss intensive expectations, goals, and any specific tasks they need to complete

---

22 The Intensive Method Companion Workbook and The Intensive Method online course both include a comprehensive journaling exercise to support the development of your intake system. Visit theintensivemethod.com to learn more.

before the intensive. This call (or email, or in-person time) should happen after the screening call but with enough time prior to the start of the intensive for your client to act upon any tasks they need to complete.

Checklists for Clients and Clinicians: Create detailed checklists for both clients and clinicians outlining pre-intensive tasks and preparations. This can help ensure that all necessary steps are taken and nothing is overlooked.[23]

Interdisciplinary Collaboration: If you are working with a team, establish effective communication and collaboration systems between clinicians, support staff, and any other professionals involved in the intensive.

Resource Materials: Compile and organize resource materials, worksheets, or therapeutic tools that will be used during the intensive. Having these materials ready in advance can save time during the sessions.

Tools That Make It Work

Once you have gathered together all of the content you want your clients to complete prior to the intensive, it's time to map out how you want to collect the information. You can set up your communications many different ways—through an online course system, using fillable PDFs attached to emails, through online forms embedded in your website, or even through mailed packets—the mode you choose is really up to you and your comfort level.

The system we use right now aims to keep all necessary paperwork and onboarding information in one communication, which is our intensive onboarding email. This email includes:

- the intensive date and time confirmation
- intake documents and assessments
- additional agreements

In the future, we plan to move our onboarding process to an online course platform that will utilize explainer videos, embedded links, and downloadable resources to guide clients through the intake process.

There are lots of tools out there to help you streamline your systems electronically. Keep in mind that all of these are tools that can help you, but

---

23 *An Administrative Intensive Checklist Spreadsheet is available through The Intensive Method online course and can also be downloaded from theintensivemethod.com.*

that does not mean they are necessary for your practice. If you are a technophile, then you might love this whole list and start shopping this afternoon for apps and software programs that can make your life easier.

But if you are a technophobe, well, you might want to just skip this section. Whether technophile or technophobe, you'll need to decide what will work best for your practice.

Here are a few ideas to inspire you:

Online Intake Forms: Create electronic intake forms that clients can complete online before the intensive. This reduces paperwork, ensures data accuracy, and allows the clinician to review information in advance.

Client Portals: Use secure client portals for document sharing, including consent forms, pre-assessment questionnaires, and any necessary educational materials. This promotes a centralized and organized information exchange.

Appointment Scheduling Apps: Implement appointment scheduling apps that allow clients to book and manage appointments online. These tools can sync with the clinician's calendar and send automated reminders to both parties.

Automated Reminders and Communications: Set up automated reminders for clients leading up to the intensive. Additionally, use automated communication tools to share essential information, such as session agendas, preparation tasks, and any required readings.

Teletherapy Platforms: Utilize secure teletherapy platforms for virtual sessions during the intensive. These platforms often include features such as video conferencing, chat, and document sharing, facilitating seamless communication.

Collaborative Document Editing: Use cloud-based collaborative document editing tools to work on treatment plans, goals, and other documents in real-time with clients. This fosters collaboration and ensures that everyone has access to the most up-to-date information.

Task Management Apps: Implement task management apps to create and share checklists for both clients and clinicians. This helps everyone stay organized and on track with pre-intensive preparations.

Virtual Whiteboards or Mind Mapping Tools: Use virtual whiteboards or mind mapping tools during planning sessions to visually organize thoughts, goals, and strategies. This can enhance collaboration and provide a dynamic way to structure discussions.

Electronic Treatment Planning Software: Explore electronic treatment planning software that allows clinicians to develop, update, and share treatment plans digitally. This can facilitate collaboration and ensure that plans are easily accessible.

Secure Messaging Platforms: Incorporate secure messaging platforms for asynchronous communication between sessions. This allows clients to ask questions, share updates, or seek clarification, promoting ongoing engagement.

Electronic Payment Systems: Implement electronic payment systems for handling billing and payments. This simplifies financial transactions and reduces administrative burden.

Data Analytics and Progress Tracking Tools: Utilize data analytics and progress tracking tools to monitor client progress over time. These tools can provide valuable insights into the effectiveness of interventions and guide ongoing planning.

Automation for Administrative Tasks: Explore automation tools for routine administrative tasks, such as sending session notes, processing invoices, or updating client records. This can free up time for more meaningful therapeutic work.

Feedback Surveys and Assessment Tools: Integrate electronic feedback surveys and assessment tools to gather client input and measure progress. This information can inform ongoing planning and adjustments to the therapeutic approach.

There's SO much out there that can help you run your practice more efficiently! A lot of the resources and automation systems we've talked about aren't practical for our practice, but you might find them to be valuable for yours. Remember, you don't have to implement everything listed above—start with the basics of what you need to do to get your practice up and running, and then incorporate the tools and systems you need to support you as you grow.

Streamlining the Pipeline

Once you have identified all of the information you need to collect from your clients and thought through which tools you'll use to collect that information, the next step is to define the workflow for that process. This system needs to be clear and simple to save you and your clients (and your support staff, if you have them) from days of headaches. You might take all that you have gathered in the previous sections and draft a map of your intake process. What will your clients do first? Second? Third? What will *you* do first, second, and third?

Efficient systems depend on staying organized so that you can easily log, edit, and reference the information after it comes in. So how do you manage client information, scheduling appointments, and coordinating logistics effectively? Here are a few more tools that can help you streamline your process.

Use Electronic Health Records (EHR) Software: This certainly isn't a requirement, but implementing EHR software to centralize and organize client information can streamline documentation, securely store records, and facilitate easy access to relevant client data, especially as your practice grows.

You do not have to have EHR software in order to do an intensive. Personally, I have never used an EHR system because I was able to set up my own system that worked well for me. So far, I have not found an EHR that is targeted for intensive therapy, so despite the potential benefits of that system, it is not imperative to pay for expensive programs to run intensives.

Implement a Centralized Scheduling System: Use a centralized scheduling system to manage appointments. Rather than just sending an event confirmation, consider sending a calendar invitation to your client's email. This ensures that your calendar and your client's calendars are synchronized, reducing the chance of scheduling conflicts and facilitating efficient coordination. Just a note here, though, you do want to respect your client's confidentiality and they may not like that option. So be sure to think that through, if that is something that your clients would want you to consider.

Set Up Automated Reminders: You can save yourself a lot of time by implementing an automated reminder system for clients leading up to the intensive. Reminders can include details about the schedule, preparation instructions, and any necessary paperwork.

Create Client Folders or Digital Profiles: Organize client information into individual folders or digital profiles. This could include a summary of treatment plans, progress notes, process notes, or any relevant assessments.

Develop a Secure Communication System: Use secure communication channels for exchanging sensitive information with clients, ensuring confidentiality and compliance with privacy regulations.

Establish Efficient Billing and Payment Processes: Implement efficient billing processes, including the use of billing software. Clearly communicate payment policies and provide multiple payment options for clients.

Utilize Secure Cloud Storage: Store digital documents securely using cloud storage solutions. This enhances accessibility, collaboration, and data security.

As you develop your system for managing intake, find what works best for you and make sure you're in compliance with HIPAA regulations. Automate as much as possible to save time.

It's important as clinicians that we stay relevant and in the modern era so we are able to offer our clients ways to add efficiency and convenience when possible. A clear, systematic approach to intake will build trust and establish clear expectations for your intensive, which will only enhance your client's experience when they arrive at your site.

CHAPTER 16

Treatment Planning That Works

Now that you've collected information from your client in the onboarding process, it's time to make the magic happen! Goal setting and treatment planning are cornerstones to an effective intensive experience. In this chapter, we'll go over how to customize the treatment plan template you've developed as part of your 3-day intensive structure based on the material you've collected from your client. We'll also talk about the importance of client collaboration in planning and review several tools you can use to enhance this process.

Building a Strong Foundation: Customizing Templates Based on Intake

In my practice, I have designed several different intensives to address very specific goals. Those intensives have a set treatment plan template I use as my basis for planning, adapting as needed to accommodate my client's various needs.

When I began, I started with just one primary intensive targeted for couples entering betrayal recovery together. I have expanded to many other types of intensive templates over the years. You too will have the option to keep it simple and stick to one or two, or you could also develop many variations and custom-tailored options.

As I said earlier on, if you're just starting out, I recommend using the Build-Measure-Learn framework to develop your first intensive. Build a Minimum Viable Product (MVP) that has just enough features to test out your intensive. Keep it simple and flexible, even if you have big dreams of more sophisticated or complex intensives. From that initial intensive concept, you can then test your design with a couple of clients, analyze your offering, and either pivot (change direction) or persevere (keep improving what's working).

Now, just because you are picking one area of focus, doesn't mean it's one size fits all. For example, in my practice I utilize the phase of recovery my clients are in to determine which intensive structure I employ. If they are in the first phase, they receive a Foundations Intensive that focuses on immediate safety, initial boundaries, and best practices for recovery. If someone is in the third or fourth phase of recovery, I might offer them a more advanced intensive that focuses on complex trauma, making amends, or therapy goals that are aligned with a more strategic coaching approach.

I have found this structure to be very effective. However, it took a lot of trial-and-error structuring and restructuring, running various iterations of these intensives, and receiving client feedback to arrive at these well-established intensives. It may take some experimenting with your program before you settle into this kind of a groove, and that's perfectly fine!

Therapy is a science and an art... with The Intensive Method, you have many tools and resources to give you as much structure and order to your intensive as possible. If you follow the guidelines we've outlined in this book and if you have downloaded some or all of the resources we've provided through the website, you shouldn't have to go through too many rounds of trial and error. We have tested and used the tools and resources with clients for many years now.

What you *will* want to test and measure is your own specific offering, the flow and structure you've established, and the experience your clients take away with them. Just keep in mind that during every intensive, you will learn a lot. Each iteration will help you for future iterations.

Even though you will invest a lot of time and energy into defining the structure of your intensive treatment plan, it doesn't need to be public information. My clients aren't aware of this behind-the-scenes structure, and yours won't need to be either. This is part of what makes our secret sauce so powerful.

Although the system and treatment plans are very similar from client-to-client, no therapeutic intensive is ever the same. Begin with a strong foundational framework and hone your craft as you go along, and your clients will feel personally cared for and changed by the powerful intensive experience.

Collaborative Goal Setting Leading Up to the Intensive

Even if you have a set structure that you typically follow for each client and you generally know what goals you are able to achieve during these sessions, it is still important to involve your client in the goal setting process.

Collaborative Goal Setting: This is your client's therapeutic intensive experience. The best outcomes are made possible through collaborative goal setting. You can begin this process on your screening call or incorporate it as part of your onboarding process.

As you work together during the intensive, you should continue to foster a sense of empowerment and autonomy with regards to their goals. Encourage them to take an active role in shaping and pursuing their goals.

Establish Rapport: From the beginning of your relationship with your client, you want to work to build a strong therapeutic alliance with them. A trusting relationship is essential for goal setting.

Assessment and Understanding: Use the assessments you've received from your client to get a thorough understanding about their background, history, strengths, challenges, values, and preferences. You want to understand why your client is seeking out therapy and what they hope to achieve.

Clarify Client's Values and Priorities: Either as part of your onboarding process or when your client first arrives for their intensive, discuss with your client their core values and priorities in life. This is an important consideration: you want to outline goals that align with your client's values.

Cultural Sensitivity: Like core values and priorities, it's also important to take into consideration your client's cultural background, so that the goals you map out align with their cultural context and beliefs.

Set Realistic Expectations: You and your client will both be surprised how quickly three days goes by. It is important that your client understands what can be accomplished realistically within the concentrated timeframe you're together.

Prioritize Goals: There might be a lot the client hopes to achieve during your intensive, so it's up to you to help them set appropriate expectations. You can do this by helping them prioritize their goals, addressing the most pressing issues first.

Explore Short- and Long-Term Goals: There are some goals you can achieve in the short-term setting of an intensive, whereas other goals may require ongoing effort over a much longer timespan. You can help your client set appropriate goals for the couple of days you have together, and later, as part of their ongoing treatment plan, you can help them map out ways to achieve their long-term goals. By the end of the intensive, your client should have a clear picture of what they need to do in order to continue their recovery beyond the time they've spent with you.

Incorporating Goals into Your Intensive Treatment Plan

Goal setting plays a crucial role in informing your treatment plan. Goals serve as a roadmap for therapy, guiding the therapeutic process in a purposeful and client-centered manner.

Once you have defined your client's goals, you can focus on specific areas of concern or change. In my practice, a client's goals determine which structured intensive I want to "pull off the shelf."

Tailored Interventions: A client's goals and the severity of their symptoms inform the selection of appropriate therapeutic interventions. You should have some basic interventions ready to cover content for the intensive, but you can also use your client's goals to decide which techniques and approaches you think will be most effective, adding in additional interventions when appropriate. This is where the wealth of options we discussed in Part 3 can come into play.

One of the joys of intensives is the freedom and flexibility you have to explore a variety of therapeutic techniques that aren't as feasible during traditional therapy sessions. Identify for yourself the tools you already have in your therapeutic toolkit; you'll likely discover that you have a lot more available to you to explore in an intensive setting than you realize! Intensives are a great opportunity to take the training manuals off the shelf and find things you've always wanted to try with clients but have been too busy to play with... until now!

Prioritization: The priorities you learned about in the goal setting process will help you prioritize issues to address during therapy. Your treatment plan can be structured to address the most pressing concerns first, ensuring a strategic and effective approach.

Documentation and Progress Tracking: From the beginning, keep clear and concise records of the goals set and the progress your client has made, so that you can use this information to adjust the treatment plan.

How to Structure Your Intensive Treatment Plan

The contents of your treatment plan are going to vary based on the type of therapy you provide. There are several different ways you can go about structuring your treatment plan. Let's walk through one such structure for a 3-day intensive therapy session.

You'll recall that we already covered this structure in an earlier chapter, but now we'll see what's "behind the curtain" and talk about how the treatment plan aligns with this schedule.

Day One

Day 1 of the intensive will begin with relationship building, followed by a comprehensive assessment. Based on the outcomes of the assessment, spend the afternoon collaborating and documenting the goals and expectations for the intensive with your client.

You will also provide relevant psychoeducation about the therapeutic approach and interventions you plan to use during the rest of the intensive. Remind your client about the importance of self-reflection and active participation in the process to help them prepare mentally and emotionally for Day 2.

Here is an example of what you might cover on Day 1:

GOAL: *Review Trauma History*

INTERVENTION: *Create a Trauma Egg on Whiteboard*

PSYCHOEDUCATION: *Show Video on PTSD and Explain EMDR*

Day Two, Morning

Based on the goals you established with your client, implement therapeutic interventions that are tailored to those goals in the morning session. You'll explore key themes and patterns related to the client's concerns during this time as well as provide feedback on your client's observations and themes.

GOAL: *Process Client's Trauma Egg*

THERAPEUTIC INTERVENTION: *Add SUDS Scale to Life Events and Cognitions*

CLIENT OBSERVATIONS: *Take Note of Increased Anxiety and Emotional*

Dysregulation, Counterbalanced with a Sense of Hope for the Future

PROCESS: *Identify Other Traumatic Memories for Future Aftercare*

Day Two, Afternoon

In the afternoon session, you'll build on the morning's work, addressing deeper issues and exploring potential solutions, using a variety of therapeutic modalities as appropriate. Make sure you schedule some time to process the morning session and prepare for the afternoon session.

In addition to more therapy work, take time in the afternoon to help your client integrate any insights they've experienced into their daily life. Their time with you ends soon, but you'll want them to take reflective exercises or homework back to their accommodations after your session ends. This will help to reinforce therapeutic gains that were made throughout the day.

GOAL: *Focus on Additional Interventions and More Psychoeducation Regarding EMDR*

INTERVENTION: *EMDR Processing Session*

INTEGRATION: *Post-Process Journaling and Reflection of Insights and Experience*

HOMEWORK: *Journal, Prepare for Final Day*

Day Three, Morning

The final day of the intensive is all about integrating the content that has been covered over the last two days into a recovery or treatment plan the client can take with them into the future.

In the morning session, spend time reviewing the progress they've made during the intensive, reflecting on changes, insights, and challenges that have come up. You'll want to prepare your client for reentry—sure, it's only been a couple of days, but those couple of days have been intense. How can they sustain the gains they've made in the last few days? Offer your client different coping mechanisms and strategies they can employ when faced with potential challenges in their regular life.

INSIGHTS AND OBSERVATIONS: *Process Homework and Finish EMDR Process*

CHALLENGES: *Discuss Client Concerns and Potential Threats and Triggers*

COPING MECHANISMS / STRATEGIES: *Provide Skills, Tools, and Resources*

Day Three, Afternoon

The afternoon session is a time to recap and celebrate the gains your client has made over the last three days. After reviewing the goals the client had during the intensive, now is a great time to discuss future goals and potential ongoing therapy options. You'll work together with your client to develop a post-intensive plan, including follow-up sessions or resources.

CLIENT GAINS: *Deepen Insight and Understanding by Reviewing Client Observations*

FUTURE GOALS: *Set Goals in Writing*

FUTURE TREATMENT RECOMMENDATIONS: *Discuss Ongoing Treatment Strategy and Schedule First Aftercare*

POST-INTENSIVE PLAN: *Discuss Ongoing Feedback Process and Collaboration with Other Clinicians*

Making Adjustments on the Fly

There's lots of room in this framework for you to adapt and adjust your particular area of expertise, but even once you've solidified how your intensives will go, there will always be times when you need to make adjustments as you're working with your client in the intensive setting. Your ability to remain flexible is important!

Incorporate regular reviews of your client's goals and solicit client feedback throughout the intensive to assess progress. It's possible, even in such a short period of time, that their goals might need to be adjusted based on their evolving needs and insights throughout the intensive.

There also may come a point during the intensive when obstacles or barriers arise that get in the way of your client's ability to achieve the goals they've identified. You'll want to develop strategies to overcome these challenges. We'll discuss ways you can navigate challenging moments during intensives in Part 6.

Your treatment plan from the intensive will continue to evolve in future aftercare meetings with your client based on how they are progressing toward their goals and how their circumstances have changed.

It is important to keep a feedback loop running between you and your client, even after the intensive is over, to inform their ongoing treatment plan and stay connected. Between aftercare sessions, ask follow-up questions or simply check in to give your clients additional opportunities to communicate their goals and progress.

Keep in mind if you are a licensed clinician, and your clients are out of the state in which you are licensed, these communications would be considered consultations, not therapy sessions.

Customizing Clinician Goal Setting

Like I mentioned at the beginning of this chapter, I've been able to develop and adapt a structure that works really well for my specific area of expertise, so the goal setting process is not nearly as critical to determine the framework for my intensives at this point.

You need to do what works best for you. If you have a lot of clinical experience, you may not need an extensive or formalized goal setting and treatment planning process like this. Some clinicians are more comfortable being thoroughly prepared while others prefer to handle things as they come up. The level of planning you need to do might also be contingent upon the level of care your clients need.

If there are specific considerations outside of your scope of practice, you might need to be more prepared for those as well.

Before any breakthrough can happen in your office with a client, there's essential work that takes place behind the scenes. We've covered screening your clients, gathering background information, setting goals, and shaping a container that is safe and strategic for guiding your clients into a transformative experience. Throughout Part 4, we've walked through the systems and practices that prepare clients for meaningful work. But that work doesn't stop with the client.

As we turn to Part 5, we will shift focus to *you: the clinician*. Building a sustainable intensive practice isn't just about what happens during sessions, it's about how you manage your own time, protect your energy, and structure your business to support the life and impact you want to have. Let's take a look now at what it means to design your weeks with purpose, care for yourself like a professional, and build a practice that runs smoothly behind the scenes.

PART 5

Optimizing the Intensive Practitioner's Life

CHAPTER 17

Time Management and Your Work Week

In the last section, we focused on the heart of client care—intake, assessment, and crafting a treatment plan that honors each person's goals while making the most of the intensive format. Now, we turn the lens back on *you*—the practitioner.

The work you do is meaningful and demanding, and while intensives can be incredibly rewarding, they also require intentional planning and strong boundaries to remain sustainable. That's why Part 5 is all about optimizing your practice in a way that supports both your clients' healing and your own well-being.

In this chapter, we'll explore time management strategies that go beyond productivity tips. We'll help you design a rhythm for your work week that prioritizes presence, protects your energy, and supports profitability. You'll learn how to block time for prep and recovery, schedule for sustainability, and develop a weekly flow that works for you—not just for your calendar.

This is about more than just running a practice. It's about building a life you don't need a break from.

Therapists are gifted helpers, but sometimes that gift can become a curse. We want to help ALL the people! What's one more client in an already full week? You and I both know that wringing every second out of everyday isn't a sustainable long-term strategy. If you are planning to transition gradually from traditional therapy or coaching to intensive therapy or coaching, time management is especially important.

Here are some tips to help you manage your schedule well:

Block Scheduling: Allocate specific blocks of time for intensive therapy sessions and traditional therapy sessions. This helps in maintaining focus during each type of session and avoids overlapping commitments. We'll go over this schedule in greater depth later in this chapter.

Set Clear Boundaries: Establish clear boundaries with clients (and with your staff!) regarding the scheduling of intensive therapy sessions. Make sure clients understand the time commitment involved and adhere to the agreed-upon schedule. This will protect your much-needed off-hours during an intensive.

Prioritize Tasks: Prioritize tasks based on urgency and importance. Identify critical activities such as client sessions, administrative work, and self-care, and allocate time for each accordingly. Yes, even self-care. If it isn't on the calendar, is it even a priority?

Flexible Hours: You might consider offering flexible hours for intensive therapy sessions, including evenings or weekends, to accommodate clients' schedules without compromising traditional therapy sessions. If you decide to offer intensives outside of traditional work hours, block scheduling your "off" hours will become even more important. For every weekend you spend with clients, you should make a point of blocking off a weekend's worth of time elsewhere to recuperate.

Batch Similar Tasks: Group similar tasks together to maximize efficiency. For example, dedicate specific days or times for client intake assessments, treatment planning, or documentation.

Regular Review and Adjustments: As you go along, make sure you regularly review your schedule and assess what's working well and what needs adjustment. Be flexible and willing to adapt your schedule to meet the evolving needs of your practice and your clients.

Self-Care: Don't forget to prioritize self-care to prevent burnout and maintain your well-being. I can't preach this too often! Schedule time for breaks, exercise, hobbies, and relaxation to recharge and stay energized for both intensive and traditional sessions.

Delegate Non-Essential Tasks: Delegate administrative tasks such as scheduling appointments, billing, or managing paperwork to support staff or virtual assistants. This frees up time for you to focus on client care. Delegation is often a challenge for high-performing people, so let's take some time to go over a valuable tool that can help you find clarity around delegation as well as the value of your time.

Delegation: 80/20 Your Clinical Practice

When you're used to doing everything in your practice, it can feel overwhelming to even consider asking someone else to help you. Where do you even begin?

A useful business management practice that can help you with this is the 80/20 Principle. The 80/20 Principle shows up in lots of different industries and organizations. Also known as the Pareto Principle, it's the idea that roughly 80% of the effects come from just 20% of the causes.

In business, 80% of a company's revenue tends to come from 20% of its customers.

When it comes to productivity, the principle suggests that 80% of results are generated by 20% of efforts. By identifying the most critical tasks that yield the highest impact, you are able to see where you should spend the most time, rather than spreading your efforts out evenly across all tasks.

As you transition your business from traditional services to intensive services, you can use the 80/20 Principle to sort out what tasks you've taken on that might be better off delegated to others. There are five different technical skill levels identified as part of the 80/20 Principle. Your job is to figure out what you do, how much time it takes for you to do it, and what level of technical expertise it requires. Going through this exercise provides you with clarity about the kinds of tasks you can afford to delegate to someone else and what you need to continue doing on your own.[24]

Each skill level requires different levels of responsibility, supervision, accountability, complexity, autonomy, and ability. Let's go over the five different levels of technical skills as they relate to therapists or life coaches.

Level 5 - Leading Strategic Work

As the owner, CEO, or president of a mental health practice, your focus is

---

24 *The 80/20 Worksheet for Practitioners is available through The Intensive Method online course and as a free download from theintensivemethod.com.*

on setting the long-term vision for the practice and guiding it through transitions and growth. Typical tasks at this level include:

- Setting the mission, vision, and values of the practice.
- Developing long-term strategic plans and goals.
- Identifying new opportunities for expansion or specialization.
- Establishing partnerships or collaborations with other organizations.
- Making high-level decisions regarding the direction and future of the practice.

Because of the nature of these kinds of tasks, it is unlikely that you will want to delegate any of these types of tasks. Unless you are the head of a much larger practice that has several C-suite level executives who are also responsible for the strategic vision of your company, keep these tasks in your bucket. If vision and strategy work is not your particular gifting, then consider hiring a consultant to help you establish the vision for your organization, and then move forward with execution from there.

Level 4 - Planning Strategic Work

Level 4 tasks involve translating the long-term vision set by leadership into actionable strategies. Typical tasks include:

- Conducting market analysis and identifying target demographics.
- Developing marketing strategies to promote the practice and attract clients.
- Creating business plans and budgets aligned with the overall vision.
- Designing programs or services based on client needs and market trends.
- Evaluating potential risks and developing contingency plans.

Many Level 4 tasks can and often should be considered for delegation, especially by therapists who are trying to focus their time on clinical work and preserve work-life balance. While these tasks are strategic and align with leadership vision (which means they are not always fully delegable), parts of them can be delegated to capable support professionals, such as a practice manager, marketing consultant, or virtual assistant.

Once you've charted out the kinds of tasks you are doing at this level and are ready to determine what to keep and what to delegate, you might consider following this principle: ***Delegate the research, implementation, and***

documentation. Retain the vision, final decisions, and clinical alignment.

Level 3 - Managing Operational Activities

This level involves overseeing day-to-day operations and ensuring that the practice runs smoothly. Typical tasks include:

- Managing financial activities such as budgeting, billing, and financial reporting.
- Supervising administrative staff and delegating tasks as needed.
- Handling client scheduling and appointment management.
- Monitoring and evaluating the quality of therapeutic services.
- Implementing policies and procedures to ensure compliance and efficiency.

Many of the tasks at this level of your organization are prime candidates for delegation, especially if you want to scale your business or retain more of your time and energy for clinical work. At Level 3, your job is to set expectations, review outcomes, and make high-level decisions, not to stay in the weeds of every task. ***Delegate execution. Retain leadership.***

Level 2 - Executing Operational Activities

At this level, therapists are primarily focused on delivering therapeutic services to clients. Typical tasks include:

- Conducting individual or group therapy sessions.
- Assessing clients' needs and developing treatment plans.
- Providing counseling and support to clients dealing with mental health issues.
- Documenting client progress and maintaining accurate records.
- Collaborating with other healthcare professionals as needed for client care.

Level 2 activities are centered on direct client care, which is often the core role of a therapist or coach. These tasks are less delegable, but some supporting functions around them can be streamlined or delegated to protect your time and energy for the work only you can do.

The guiding principle for Level 2 delegation is this: ***If it's clinical, keep it. If it's logistical, systematize or delegate.*** The goal isn't to offload care but to free up time and energy so you can be fully present with your clients and avoid burnout.

Level 1 - Supporting Operational Activities

Tasks at this level involve providing support to ensure the smooth functioning of day-to-day operations. Typical tasks include:

- Assisting with administrative tasks such as filing, data entry, and answering phones.
- Managing inventory and ordering supplies for the practice.
- Providing logistical support for client appointments and meetings.
- Assisting therapists with client intake processes and paperwork.
- Handling basic troubleshooting and technical support for office equipment.

Level 1 tasks are highly delegable and, in most cases, should not be handled by therapists or coaches at all. These operational support activities are essential to running a practice smoothly, but they don't require clinical expertise or high-level strategic oversight. Delegating or outsourcing these tasks is one of the quickest ways to free up your time for more valuable work at Levels 2–4.

If it doesn't require a license or clinical judgment, it likely belongs to someone else. Delegating Level 1 tasks is essential for therapists to focus on their zone of genius—client care, strategy, and meaningful growth.

How to 80/20 Your Current Week

Document the amount of time you spend and the type of tasks you do in the next week to give yourself a portrait of your typical work week using this general format:[25]

Skill Level	Current Daily Tasks & Responsibilities	Time Spent Weekly
Level 5 - Leadership		
Level 4 - Strategic Planning		

25 *The 80/20 Worksheet for Practitioners is available through The Intensive Method online course and as a free download from theintensivemethod.com.*

Skill Level	Current Daily Tasks & Responsibilities	Time Spent Weekly
Level 3 - Managing Operations		
Level 2 - Executing Operations		
Level 1 - Supporting Operations		

Once you've filled out the chart with everything that you do on a daily basis, you can begin to see the kinds of tasks that you can delegate and how much time you gain for the skills that only you (or another highly qualified therapist in your practice) can do.

What you choose to delegate will be based on your personal goals for your practice. If you want more time for clients, then you will want to hire or outsource specialists who can support your goals. If you want more time to lead and manage your practice so that it can continue to grow, then you will want to hire more therapists who can take on additional clients.

The bottom line is, you can have more time and be more productive, efficient, and satisfied in this work.

Block Scheduling for Prep, Recovery, Creativity, and Sanity

With these general time management tips in mind, let's talk about block scheduling. As a therapist transitioning into an intensive-based model, your time is no longer divided into evenly spaced weekly sessions; it's grouped into focused, immersive blocks of deep clinical work. That shift requires a new way of managing your calendar.

Enter: block scheduling.

Block scheduling is the practice of setting aside uninterrupted chunks of time in your week for specific types of work—client sessions, preparation, admin tasks, marketing, and most importantly, rest and recovery. Instead of reacting to your schedule, you proactively design it around your priorities.

Block scheduling:

- **Protects your energy.** Intensives are emotionally and mentally demanding. Without built-in recovery time, burnout is inevitable. Blocking recovery days before and after intensives ensures you can show up at your best—for both your clients and yourself.
- **Improves clinical presence.** When you know your prep time, session time, and follow-up time are clearly defined, you're able to be fully present with your clients—without distractions or unfinished tasks looming in the background.
- **Increases profitability and sustainability.** A well-structured calendar helps you see how many intensives you can realistically offer in a month while still allowing time for admin, consults, and other streams of income. This helps you price and plan your practice accordingly.
- **Supports work-life balance.** When you treat your calendar as a reflection of your values—not just a list of obligations—you can carve out time for rest, relationships, and what matters most outside of work.

To get started with block scheduling, you'll want to establish your expectations for how frequently you offer intensives and then schedule time on your calendar accordingly. I use Apple's Calendar app, but you can just as easily use Google, an appointment management system, or even an old-school desk calendar to block time. I recommend color coding your calendar by categories so that it's easy for you to see at a glance what your day or week looks like.

In a typical week for my practice, which is exclusively intensives, I have set aside three days for an intensive, plus two days of aftercare, which are reserved for people who were in an intensive sometime during the last 3-6 months.

If you plan to integrate one intensive each month, you might select a week each month to block off as available for intensives and aftercare, so that you know to avoid scheduling any other conflicts. You may have other therapy or different types of appointments, but if you have that blocked out, it will be protected.

Currently, my projected weekly schedule includes one day of administrative work, one day for aftercare, and three days for intensives. The administrative day gives me the ability to spend more time in pre- and post-prep if needed, as well as allocating time to work on the business rather than in the business. It's a good idea to consider blocking time for screening calls, other important meetings, and reminders that can easily be filled in or deleted if not needed.

For those of you that LOVE color coding and organization, you may prefer an Advanced Block Scheduling System. This system simply expands the different categories of blocks on your calendar with additional slots for future screening calls, other therapy appointments, or consultations. Advanced block scheduling is extremely helpful if you have an administrative support person that helps with billing and/or intensive coordination. This allows you to utilize your calendar for more than just planning; it can also be used to share information and serve as a tool for administrative tasks.

Time (Management) Is Money

All of this delegation work and block scheduling translates into more revenue generation in several different ways.

Efficient scheduling allows you to maximize your client capacity by minimizing gaps between appointments and ensuring that each available time slot is utilized effectively. This increases your billable hours and overall revenue. With The Intensive Method, you will be more efficient with your client load and reduce gaps by ensuring your client hours are all grouped together.

Proper scheduling practices, such as sending appointment reminders and implementing cancellation policies, can help reduce the number of no-shows and last-minute cancellations. By minimizing these occurrences, you can ensure a more consistent stream of revenue and avoid missed opportunities for billable sessions. Intensives are secured with deposits for half the intensive, so your clients are less likely to cancel. Plus, with an intensive, 18 hours are billed at once rather than 18 individual clients who all may or may not cancel.

For clinicians integrating intensives into their traditional practice, effective time management and scheduling are essential for maintaining a balanced workload. By strategically allocating time for both types of sessions, practitioners can cater to the needs of different client populations while maximizing revenue potential. This also goes for balancing reduced fee clients if you choose to offer pro bono services, sliding scale fees, or medicaid for example.

Time management practices extend beyond client appointments to include administrative tasks such as billing, documentation, and correspondence. By streamlining the number of clients each week and incorporating The Intensive

Method processes through automation, delegation, or efficient workflows, you can free up more time to focus on revenue-generating activities, such as client sessions or marketing efforts. The 80/20 chart is one tool to help you find clarity in your role so that you can work smarter, not harder.

Effective time management allows you to allocate sufficient time and resources to each client session, delivering high-quality care and maximizing the perceived value of your services. By pricing your services based on the value provided rather than solely on time spent, you can justify higher rates and increase revenue per session, not to mention the compassion fatigue that we can experience when splitting our heart and brain space between 20-30 clients per week. Imagine spending 18 hours with one client versus 18 different clients in the same time frame.

Time management includes allocating time for ongoing professional development and continuing education, which can enhance your skills and qualifications. By staying updated on the latest research, techniques, and modalities, you can attract more clients, command higher rates, and increase revenue. Utilizing the benefits of more efficient scheduling and increased revenue, you will free up more time for professional development.

Ultimately, time management practices and delegation techniques like these will help you make wise choices for your practice as you shift into offering The Intensive Method. One of the major reasons I chose to switch to intensives was to free up more time for myself and my family, and it has definitely paid off! Not only do I have more freedom in my practice, I also have more revenue. AND, my clients benefit from the concentrated time as well.

It's truly a great way to practice therapy.

Another aspect of time management that we didn't cover here is the importance of breaks and self-care practices during intensives. In the next chapter, we're going to talk about why breaks are so important, for both you and your client, how to implement a healthy rhythm in the intensive schedule, and self-care strategies you can offer your clients during intensives.

CHAPTER 18

Self-Care as a Clinical Competency

One of the major benefits of adding intensives to your practice is so you can work smarter, not harder. Many of you are interested in intensives specifically because of a key area of work/life balance you want to address. Some realize you need to maximize your time and increase overall revenue; others want to plan for retirement and have money set aside for later in life, and others still might be looking for more control over your schedule, allowing for personal priorities like travel, family, volunteering, or greater flexibility to devote to professional things like writing, speaking, supervision, or pro bono work, and so on.

Whatever the case may be, this chapter is about helping you make those dreams a reality while still doing what you love and feel called to do.

Many clinicians are others focused. They tend to over-extend themselves because they feel called to help others. This is a worthy cause but creates challenges that shouldn't be ignored.

As you're exploring intensives for your practice, it's important to ask yourself, how could offering intensives change your life for the better? Dream a little! What needs to change in your life for you to be the healthiest version of yourself?

This is an important step before we tackle the tough topic of taking breaks and self-care practices.

And it is a tough topic. Take Joe for example. Joe is a colleague of mine who pushed himself hard. One day, he found himself in the hospital with more questions than answers. He needed a 9-week sabbatical from work, felt in a fog most of the time, and had no income during that period. Joe hadn't anticipated what compassion fatigue might do to him.

Like Joe, many don't realize the toll that work is taking until it's too late and some set of consequences has already set in. Joe told me later that he wished he had taken more time to consider himself. As the saying goes, when you are in an airplane and the oxygen masks drop, you need to put yours on first before assisting others.

We have to practice what we promote to our clients. You must begin with yourself and your own self-care.

Rest Is an Imperative

Before we talk about how to integrate breaks into your intensives and strategies for self-care, let's start with *why*. Anecdotally, we know that rest is necessary for both you and your client's well-being. Yeah, yeah, we say, rest is important for *you*, but *I* can power through.

If we want our clients to be healthy and balanced, shouldn't we strive to be healthy and balanced too? Your heart and brain need a break, both during intensive therapy sessions and beyond. Intensive therapy sessions can be emotionally draining for both the therapist and the client. Taking breaks allows you to recharge, regulate your emotions, and maintain focus throughout the session, ensuring that both parties can engage effectively in the therapeutic process.

Breaks also provide an opportunity for both the therapist and the client to reflect on the content of the session and integrate the insights gained. This reflection time can help deepen the therapeutic work and promote greater understanding and insight into the issues being addressed.

Therapists often deal with heavy emotional content during intensive therapy sessions, which can lead to burnout if you don't take adequate breaks to care for yourself. By taking breaks, therapists can prevent burnout and maintain their emotional resilience, which is essential for providing quality care to their clients over the long term.

Breaks help establish and maintain boundaries between the therapist and the client, ensuring that both parties have time for self-care and maintaining a healthy therapeutic relationship.

Finally, breaks provide an opportunity for both the therapist and the client to engage in self-care practices such as deep breathing, mindfulness exercises, or simply taking a walk. These practices can help individuals manage stress and anxiety and promote overall well-being.

Pro Tips for Your Personal Rhythm of Rest

Before we look at tips for scheduling breaks into your intensives themselves, let's talk about some ways to take care of yourself during your regular weekly, monthly, and annual routines.

Here are a few ideas and suggestions based off things I have learned over the years:

First, as a rule, I try to take off work with clients at least one week per quarter. Those weeks might be used for a vacation, a staycation, or perhaps professional development, but no matter what the alternative activity, I give myself a mental break from clinical hours and shift my rhythm. Even if you plan regular vacations and holidays, these additional four weeks are for you and can become extremely valuable for your self-care. The increased revenue from offering intensives made it possible for me. It can do the same for you.

Second, when attending an event for professional development or continuing education, I try to go in-person whenever possible, so I can network with other professionals, which candidly is often more valuable to me than the training I am attending.

These events can be good opportunities to combine work and play. Consider staying at a hotel or retreat center while doing your training. Go a few days early, or better yet, find a clinical study buddy to attend training with you so you can bounce ideas off each other, share downtime for self-care, or just let your hair down and have a little fun together. These nuanced shifts can enhance experiences so that they become multi-dimensional in purpose... learning, working, playing, *and* rest!

Now *that* is working smarter, not harder.

Don't forget to make time for personal fun at home, too! There are lots of ways to have fun, but this could be reading (and not just clinical or research reading), watching movies, going to live shows, concerts, etc. Perhaps it's time to cultivate and practice a hobby you've always wanted to pick up, like learning a new language or playing an instrument.

The bottom line is that anything a clinician would suggest to a client about living holistically and practicing good self-care is something you should be practicing yourself.

Making Time for Taking Breaks

But Cristina, you may be thinking, who has the time for all of this self-care? You do! Use your schedule blocking and categories on your calendar like we went over in the last chapter to hold space for these breaks.

This might drive you crazy, but if you really don't think you have time to take breaks for self-care, then I recommend trying out the following experiment. Feel free to use this with clients who complain about not having any free time as well.[26]

Over the course of a month, keep track of your time as follows:

Week 1 - Calendar Journal: Write down everything you did in a day or a week in a blank calendar format, but account for all your time.

Week 2 - Categorize Tasks: Categorize what you did for the day or week before and calculate totals for each category, making sure every hour goes somewhere, even if the category was downtime or free time, so you can see how you (or your client) spent time, and how much free time there really is available.

Week 3 - Map Out Your Preferred, Ideal Schedule: Use the same template but this time create a preferred and more ideal schedule. Consider your priorities and preferences, and map out the ideal preferred day or week ahead. Be sure every hour is accounted for, and add up the totals for each category to check that it's more aligned with your preferences.

Week 4 - Practice Your Schedule: Put your schedule into practice for a day or a week and assess if your priorities and calendar align. The idea here is to work your schedule the way you might work a budget. You take what you have, align and allocate based on priority, then hold yourself accountable. These exercises are good for anyone who finds themselves out of balance and are a good check for anyone, but especially individuals who have recently navigated

---

26 *A Time Blocking template is available as part of The Intensive Method online course and is available for download from theintensivemethod.com.*

a transition in their lives.

This practice will help you take control of—or take radical responsibility for—the way you spend your time and the outcomes you truly desire. By taking radical responsibility for how you spend your time, you can align the things you say you value—like self-care and rest—with your behaviors.

The Neuroscience of Rest

But what about an intensive? Your clients are paying for an intensive experience; shouldn't you pack the schedule full with as much therapy as possible so they feel like they are getting their money's worth?

Of course not. We know intuitively that the body, mind, and spirit need breaks.

Neuroscience backs up the importance of rest when it comes to integrating new ideas and practices, which is a significant aspect of the intensive experience. It turns out that our systems are designed with an operating system that benefits from breaks.

Rest plays a vital role in facilitating neuroplasticity, which is the brain's ability to reorganize itself by forming new neural connections. During rest, particularly during sleep, the brain consolidates and strengthens newly acquired information and memories, promoting learning and memory formation, all of which leads to better retention and recall.

Rest also allows for synaptic pruning, a process where weak or unnecessary connections between neurons are eliminated, while stronger connections are reinforced. This pruning process optimizes neural circuitry, enhancing cognitive function and efficiency in processing information.

Rest helps regulate neurotransmitter levels in the brain, including dopamine, serotonin, and norepinephrine, which are essential for cognitive function, mood regulation, and learning. Adequate rest ensures optimal neurotransmitter balance, promoting mental clarity, focus, and emotional well-being.

Rest allows the brain to conserve energy and replenish its resources, particularly glycogen stores, which are essential for sustaining cognitive function and neural activity. During restful periods, metabolic waste products are cleared from the brain, promoting tissue repair and rejuvenation.

Rest activates the parasympathetic nervous system, promoting relaxation and reducing stress hormone levels such as cortisol. Chronic stress impairs cognitive function and hinders the brain's ability to process and integrate new information effectively. Restful periods help counteract the negative effects of stress on the brain and support optimal cognitive function.

Rest promotes divergent thinking and creative insight by allowing the brain to make novel associations and connections between disparate ideas. During periods of rest, the brain enters a state of diffuse mode processing, where it explores alternative solutions and generates innovative ideas unconstrained by focused attention.

For all of these reasons, you and your clients need to be able to take time to let your brains do the hard work of integrating all of the new information acquired in the concentrated time you spend together.

The Perfect Break

But how long should you break? And when? What is the ideal rhythm for your clients?

According to a data deep-dive into 5.5 million daily logs by the productivity app DeskTime, the 10% most productive workers engage in job-related tasks for 52 minutes, and then take a 17-minute break. The 15-to-20 minute break is long enough for your brain to disengage and leave you feeling refreshed, but not so long that you lose focus and derail momentum from what you were doing.[27]

Rhythm and Tips for Scheduling Breaks

Even if this isn't the rhythm that you implement with your practice (and most of the time, it isn't the exact schedule I follow either), the principle stands. If you have a 45-minute session, provide a 15-minute break before you start up again. If you are going to hold a 2.5-hour long marathon session in the morning, make sure to break it up with at least two opportunities to step away, recharge, and refresh before continuing with the therapy session.

I've been practicing intensives long enough now that I don't chisel in stone times for breaks. We hold a 3-hour morning session and a 3-hour afternoon

---

27 *https://time.com/3518053/perfect-break/*

session with a 90-minute lunch in between, but I encourage my clients to ask for a break if they need them, and sometimes I will ask for a 5-10 minute break myself during a session.

The 90-minute lunch is an important block of time. Not only do you both need a little downtime to eat, but you also need that time to get grounded, and it gives your clients time to take care of any messages that may have come their way during your session with them.

Of course, the beauty of intensives is that you can customize them however you want! Start with a schedule that feels right to you and then tweak and adjust as you go along. You can be flexible and responsive to your needs as well as your client's needs throughout the session, too.

Self-Care Tips for Your Client

Your client might not be used to practicing good self-care. An intensive is a prime opportunity for them to try out some potentially new habits that can enhance their experience while they're with you and carry forward into their regular lives back home.

Here are some great tools you can give your clients to practice while they are with you:

Mindfulness and Meditation: Encourage your clients to practice mindfulness and meditation techniques to help them stay present and manage stress during the intensive sessions. Guided mindfulness exercises, deep breathing techniques, or body scans can be beneficial.

Physical Activity: Suggest incorporating physical activity into their schedule, such as going for a walk, practicing yoga, or engaging in other forms of exercise. Physical activity can help reduce stress, boost mood, and promote overall well-being. I often encourage my clients to do some stretching throughout the day at the least to get the blood flowing and muscles loosened.

Journaling: Journaling is a big part of my intensives. I highly recommend having your clients journal three times a day—morning, noon, and night—during their intensive. I give them three short and simple questions to answer:

1. **What happened?**
2. **What are you thinking?**
3. **What are you feeling?**

Writing can be a therapeutic outlet for processing emotions, gaining insight, and tracking progress throughout the therapy process.

Creative Expression: You might recommend that your clients engage in creative activities such as art, music, or writing poetry as a form of self-expression and emotional release during the intensive. (This is intended to be an unguided activity they might practice during their downtime, separate from or in addition to whatever organized, expressive therapy you may incorporate into your therapy sessions.) Creative expression can help clients explore their feelings and experiences in a nonverbal way.

Healthy Lifestyle Choices: While they are with you, don't forget to emphasize the importance of maintaining a balanced diet, staying hydrated, getting enough sleep, and avoiding substances like alcohol and drugs that can negatively impact their mental health.

Relaxation Techniques: You might want to teach clients relaxation techniques such as progressive muscle relaxation, guided imagery, or aromatherapy to help them unwind and reduce tension between sessions.

Nature Exposure: Suggest spending time outdoors in nature, whether it's taking a walk in the park, gardening, or simply enjoying the sights and sounds of nature. Nature exposure has been shown to reduce stress and improve mood.

Spiritual Practices: For clients who are open to it, exploring spiritual practices such as prayer, meditation, or attending religious services can provide comfort, meaning, and a sense of connection. Encourage those who are spiritual to lean into those practices during this time.

Stand Out from the Rest

I keep extra things in the clinician's office to support my client's self-care during their intensive. I used to have one client that came every week for the rice crispy treats I kept in my office. These extra little touches, like providing drinks and snacks in the office, can make a big difference with just a little extra investment. It can make your practice stand out, it provides a higher level of care, and it also models good self-care for the client.

You might also consider investing in and providing branded journals, pens, snacks, and sunglasses for clients to pick up in your lobby. You can simultaneously promote self-care and promote your business this way, and they also become a perk for your clinicians if you provide them to your team.

Beyond scheduling, self-care, and breaks, there are other ways you can optimize your practice to support the successful execution of an intensive therapy session. How you structure your practice matters. Let's take a look at your infrastructure and some tools that can help you.

CHAPTER 19

Business Infrastructure and Tools

In an intensive therapy service, several different areas of business are crucial for effective operation and client satisfaction. That doesn't mean you need to hire someone for each of these roles. If you are a solo entrepreneur, you are the one holding all of the hats. If you are a large group practice, you might have multiple staff members you hire to cover various roles. Regardless of how many people you have working for you, all of these roles need to be filled in one way or the other. Let's talk about each of these roles, and then we'll talk about the different ways you can meet each of these needs.

We covered strategies for delegation and scheduling in Chapter 17, which focused exclusively on your own position in order to help you find more time and space in your schedule. If you are a solo entrepreneur, *don't skip this section.* The following can still provide you with clarity and creative solutions to open up release valves in your practice, so that you are able to grow with confidence and support.

Essential Roles in Your Practice

Therapy, Coaching, or Other Mental Health Service: This is the most obvious role needed in your practice. Someone needs to provide therapeutic sessions and deliver the core services of the intensive program. This person conducts assessments, develops treatment plans, facilitates sessions, and monitors client progress, and probably, this person is you.

Administration: Administration is the management of day-to-day operations of the intensive therapy service, including scheduling appointments, coordinating client intake and discharge processes, managing paperwork and documentation, handling billing and payments, and ensuring compliance with regulatory requirements.

Marketing: Marketing the intensive therapy program to potential clients and referral sources might include developing marketing materials, managing online presence (website, social media), organizing outreach events, networking with other professionals, and cultivating referral relationships.

Customer Service: Client communications, like answering inquiries, scheduling appointments, and addressing concerns or feedback, is essential for building trust and rapport with clients and ensuring a positive experience throughout their engagement with the intensive therapy service.

Finance: Budgeting, invoicing, tracking expenses, reconciling accounts, and preparing financial reports ensures the financial health and sustainability of your business.

Quality Assurance: Quality assurance might include conducting program evaluations, collecting client feedback, monitoring outcomes, identifying areas for improvement, and implementing quality improvement initiatives to enhance the overall service delivery.

IT Support/Technology: Your business will also need technology infrastructure and technical support to ensure smooth operation of any electronic health records (EHR) systems, teletherapy platforms, scheduling software, and other digital tools.

Legal and Compliance: There will be times when you need guidance on legal and regulatory matters affecting your practice, including licensing requirements, insurance coverage, informed consent procedures, confidentiality policies, and compliance with healthcare laws (e.g., HIPAA). This service is most likely provided by lawyers represented by malpractice insurance.

Even if one person is filling multiple roles in an intensive service, acknowledging and addressing the responsibilities associated with each role is essential for maintaining operational efficiency, delivering high-quality services, and meeting the needs of clients while safeguarding the integrity of the practice.[28]

---

28 *A Roles and Responsibilities Allocation Chart is included with The Intensive Method online course and is available for download from theintensivemethod.com.*

How to Meet All of These Needs

Again, it's possible that you are the person who is *responsible* for all of these things, but that doesn't mean you need to do all of these things yourself. You can develop creative strategies to meet these needs by handing off some of those hats to other folks.

Obviously, you can hire additional support full-time or part-time, but you can also outsource certain functions to third-party service providers, utilize freelance or contract workers, partner with other professionals, implement automation and technology tools covered in Chapter 15, or seek guidance from consultants or advisors who can tailor their services to your specific needs. Be creative! Just because you aren't ready to hire someone full-time doesn't mean you can't get any help at all.

Building Your Infrastructure

There's more to think about beyond the roles your business requires; your therapy service needs a whole infrastructure to operate well and to ensure a positive experience for your clients. We've covered some of this previously but it bears repeating. Here are some essential components of the infrastructure needed for an intensive therapy service:

Physical Space: A suitable physical space is essential for conducting therapy sessions and providing a comfortable and safe environment for clients. This may include therapy rooms equipped with appropriate furniture, lighting, and privacy features to facilitate therapeutic interactions. Don't forget to enhance your physical space and therapy office with experiential tools, like toys, stuffed animals, playdough, paint, paper, colored pencils, fidget toys, coloring pages, instruments, yoga mats, feeling pillows, and so on.[29] If you choose to do your intensives in a temporary space, like a hotel suite, having an Intensive in a Box might be a good idea.[30]

Technology and Equipment: Utilize technology and equipment to

---

29 *A Therapeutic Experiential Tools List is included in The Intensive Method online course and is available for download from theintensivemethod.com.*

30 *The Intensive in a Box is a comprehensive guide to prepare and pack for an offsite intensive. It is available in The Intensive Method online course or for download from theintensivemethod.com.*

support therapy delivery, communication, and administrative tasks. This may include computers or tablets for electronic health records (EHR) and documentation, teletherapy platforms for remote sessions, audiovisual equipment for presentations or group therapy sessions, and office equipment such as printers and copiers.

Communication Systems: Implement reliable communication systems to facilitate interactions with clients, staff, and external stakeholders. This may include phone systems, email accounts, messaging platforms, and video conferencing tools for teletherapy sessions or virtual meetings.

Data Management Systems: Maintain secure and efficient systems for managing client records, scheduling appointments, and handling administrative tasks. This may involve using practice management software or electronic health record (EHR) systems to streamline workflows, track client information, and ensure compliance with data privacy regulations such as HIPAA.

Safety and Security Measures: Implement safety and security measures to protect clients, staff, and property. This may include measures such as installing security cameras, maintaining emergency procedures and protocols, ensuring compliance with building codes and safety regulations, and safeguarding sensitive information through data encryption and access controls.

Administrative Support: Establish administrative processes and support systems to manage client intake, scheduling, billing, and other operational tasks. This may involve hiring administrative staff or utilizing technology solutions such as scheduling software, billing platforms, and online payment systems to streamline administrative workflows and improve efficiency.[31]

Quality Assurance and Continuous Improvement: Develop mechanisms for monitoring and evaluating the quality of services provided and identifying areas for improvement. This may include collecting client feedback, conducting program evaluations, participating in clinical supervision or peer consultation, and implementing quality improvement initiatives based on best practices and evidence-based guidelines.

Collaborative Networks and Referral Resources: Build collaborative networks with other healthcare providers, community organizations, and

---

31 *An Administrative Intensive Checklist Spreadsheet template is included in The Intensive Method online course and is available for download from theintensivemethod.com.*

referral sources to enhance the scope and effectiveness of the intensive therapy service. This may involve establishing referral pathways, coordinating care with external providers, and participating in multidisciplinary teams or networks to support holistic client care.

Protecting Your Practice

You've got your roles and you've got your infrastructure, now, how do you keep it safe? It's important to protect your practice and your clients. The guidelines and expectations for The Intensive Method are really the same as your traditional therapy practice.

You will want to make sure these five areas are covered in your practice:

- Legal Entity Selection
- Insurance Coverage
- Professional Memberships
- Regulatory Compliance
- Risk Management

I highly recommend consulting with a legal professional to ensure your business is protected.[32]

I know that many of us didn't become therapists to also become business managers, which is why I believe it's so important to cover these various components of your practice. Getting clarity around the roles and responsibilities required to operate efficiently and effectively is a vital step in managing your intensive practice. Defining these roles, identifying how they will be managed, and protecting your business all contribute to preserving your own sanity and ensuring your success.

In our last chapter about optimizing your business (and life), we'll talk about ways you can enhance client outcomes and increase revenue through the development of client resources and workbooks.

---

32 *A Legal and Compliance Tip Sheet is included in The Intensive Method online course and is available for download from theintensivemethod.com.*

CHAPTER 20

Developing Client Resources and Workbooks

Susan arrived for her 3-day intensive anxious, scattered, and carrying a stack of scribbled notes from previous sessions with other therapists. Her clinician welcomed her, sat her down, and began reviewing goals, but throughout the day, Susan kept losing focus—asking to pause and take notes, getting distracted by trying to recall past homework assignments, and wondering what she was supposed to do with what she was learning. Without a clear structure or personalized tools, the intensive felt helpful but overwhelming, like drinking from a firehose with no cup to hold it all.

Now, let's imagine another beginning.

Marcus arrived for his 3-day intensive and was greeted with a customized workbook bearing his name. Inside were clearly outlined goals based on his intake, spaces for reflection, daily journaling prompts, and structured exercises he could return to between sessions. As the clinician guided him through the process, Marcus engaged more deeply, knowing there was a rhythm to the work. When the intensive ended, he left not only with insights but with a tangible roadmap to support his ongoing growth.

The difference? Custom materials don't just fill time—they create containers for transformation. You can create client resources and workbooks that enhance engagement, reinforce progress, and give your clients tools they'll return to long after the intensive ends. It isn't as difficult or time consuming as it sounds, either!

The Value of Custom Resources in an Intensive

The Intensive Method opens up a world of opportunities for delivering a personalized therapeutic experience, but that doesn't mean that each time, you need to start from scratch. With a variety of different worksheets, workbooks, and resources handy for your practice, you can quickly customize on the fly. As illustrated by the scenario above, customized resources allow you to tailor interventions specifically to the client's needs, preferences, and goals. This personalization increases the relevance and effectiveness of the therapeutic process.

Workbooks, guides, and resources also provide clients with tangible materials to reinforce the concepts you've introduced and discussed during therapy sessions. They serve as a consistent reference point that clients can revisit between sessions, helping to maintain momentum and continuity in their therapeutic journey.

Clients may not always remember or fully grasp the concepts discussed in therapy sessions, especially in particularly tense or highly emotional sessions. Having written materials allows them to review key points at their own pace and in their own time, fostering deeper understanding and integration of therapeutic insights later on, whether between your sessions, overnight, or after they've left the intensive. I encourage my clients to take a lot of notes during the intensive as well, reminding them it's six months of therapy in three days. They won't remember everything, so give them a place to keep their notes.

Likewise, providing clients with resources empowers them to take an active role in their healing process. It encourages self-reflection, self-awareness, and self-directed growth outside of therapy sessions, promoting autonomy and resilience.

Therapy workbooks and resources reinforce the learning process through various modalities such as writing exercises, journal prompts, visual aids, and worksheets. This multisensory approach can deepen understanding, promote retention, and facilitate behavioral change.

Customized resources can also extend the therapeutic process beyond the confines of the therapy room, enabling clients to continue their progress independently. They serve as tools for ongoing self-care and skill development, supporting long-term well-being. While intensive therapy can be costly, providing clients with supplementary resources can maximize the value of their investment. Workbooks and guides offer a cost-effective way to extend the benefits of therapy beyond scheduled sessions, enhancing overall therapeutic outcomes.

Prompts to Help You Come Up with Resources for Your Practice

The sky's the limit when it comes to the options available to you![33] Here are some possibilities to get you thinking:

Reflect on Common Challenges: Think about the most common challenges or issues clients bring to therapy. What recurring themes or patterns emerge in your caseload? How can you develop resources to address these challenges proactively?

Identify Strengths-Based Approaches: Consider clients' strengths, resources, and resilience factors. How can you design resources that capitalize on these strengths and empower clients to leverage them in their healing journey?

Explore Therapeutic Metaphors: Reflect on metaphors or visual imagery that resonate with clients and convey therapeutic concepts effectively. How can you translate these metaphors into workbook exercises, visual aids, or guided activities to enhance understanding and engagement?

Consider Developmental Stages: Tailor resources to the developmental stage and life circumstances of your clients. How can you adapt interventions to meet the unique needs of children, adolescents, adults, or older adults at different stages of the lifespan?

Incorporate Cultural Sensitivity: Recognize the diversity of cultural backgrounds, identities, and experiences among your clients. How can you develop resources that honor cultural diversity, promote inclusivity, and address cultural factors impacting mental health and well-being?

Integrate Mindfulness and Self-Compassion: Explore ways to integrate mindfulness practices, self-compassion exercises, and relaxation techniques into

---

33 *Journal and client workbook samples and templates are included in The Intensive Method online course and are available for download from theintensivemethod.com.*

your resources. How can you help clients cultivate present-moment awareness, self-acceptance, and emotional resilience through structured exercises and meditations?

Focus on Psychoeducation: Provide psychoeducational resources that enhance clients' understanding of mental health issues, coping strategies, and treatment approaches. How can you present complex concepts in a clear, accessible format that empowers clients to become informed partners in their own care?

Promote Goal Setting and Action Planning: Develop resources that guide clients in setting SMART (Specific, Measurable, Achievable, Relevant, Time-bound) goals and creating action plans to achieve them. How can you scaffold the goal-setting process and track progress effectively through workbook exercises and tracking tools?[34]

Harness Creative Expression: Tap into the therapeutic power of creative expression through writing, drawing, music, movement, or other expressive arts. How can you design resources that encourage clients to explore their thoughts, emotions, and experiences through creative mediums?

Address Transdiagnostic Factors: Consider transdiagnostic factors such as emotion regulation, distress tolerance, interpersonal skills, and cognitive flexibility. How can you develop resources that target these underlying processes across a range of mental health conditions and symptoms?

Practical Tips for Your Resources

This doesn't have to be overwhelming or over-involved. Here are a few tips as you begin thinking about the kinds of resources you want to develop:

- **Keep Them Simple:** You don't have to reinvent the wheel here. Even a basic worksheet with a couple of simple questions can go a long way in supporting your client's mental health journey.
- **Brand Your Resources:** Anything you make for your practice ought to have your logo, at least, but to really up your game, keep all of your materials in alignment with the branding you've established. (Circle back to Chapter 7 for help here.)

---

34 *A SMART Goal and Action Step Worksheet is included with The Intensive Method online course and is available for download from theintensivemethod.com.*

- **Take Advantage of Online Templates:** With so many great graphic design resources out there, you don't have to build from scratch. Canva, Etsy, and even other therapists offer templates galore that you can tweak and customize to suit your needs and brand without starting from scratch. We have included several different templates on our website that are ready for you to customize for your brand directly through Canva and Google Docs. Visit theintensivemethod.com to learn more.
- **Tailor to Your Client's Needs:** Just because you have a worksheet you really like doesn't mean that worksheet is appropriate for every client. Be intentional about what you provide your clients so they don't feel like they're wasting their time on a worksheet. Likewise, be selective about what you hand your client—you also don't want to overwhelm them with homework or information overload. Remember, you are creating a therapeutic experience for your client, not just an info dump.
- **Use Multisensory Approaches:** Incorporate resources that touch upon each of the four primary learning styles—visual, auditory, read/write, and kinesthetic (tactile)—so that individuals who are especially strong in one learning style are able to process the information in the way that suits them best.
- **Encourage Self-Reflection:** Your supplemental resources should help your client unlock greater self-awareness. If you give your client an assessment, provide them with the tools and questions they need to reflect on the meaning of their results, so they can integrate them into their evolving sense of self.
- **Provide Clear Instructions:** Make sure that your clients have a clear understanding of what they're supposed to do with a particular resource. Even if you explain how to use the resource during your session, it's still important to have written instructions that accompany the resource.
- **Structured Guidance:** The most simple of supplemental resources is a guide or workbook that offers structured guidance like prompts, questions, or cues to help clients organize their thoughts.
- **Encourage Application to Real Life:** Help your clients continue to make connections between the theoretical, therapeutic environment you've established in the intensive and their lives back home. Based on

the information they've learned in a particular session, what action steps can they take to implement this information?

Using Multimedia Elements

Worksheets, workbooks, reflection questions, and other paper products aren't the only way you can develop resources to enhance your client's experience.

Multimedia elements such as videos, audio recordings, images, and interactive presentations can capture clients' attention and make therapy sessions more engaging. This increased engagement can foster a deeper connection between the client and therapist and promote active participation in the therapeutic process.

Multimedia elements can facilitate visualization and symbolic representation of therapeutic concepts, emotions, and experiences. Visual aids, such as diagrams, infographics, or metaphorical images, can help clients externalize internal experiences and gain new perspectives on their challenges and strengths.

Videos, music, art, and other multimedia formats can evoke and express complex emotions in ways that words alone may not capture. By tapping into different sensory channels, therapists can help clients explore and process emotions more deeply, leading to enhanced emotional awareness and expression.

Multimedia resources can also provide opportunities for clients to practice and reinforce therapeutic skills outside of therapy sessions. For example, therapists may use audio recordings for guided relaxation or mindfulness exercises, video demonstrations for communication skills training, or interactive apps for emotion regulation practice.

Multimedia elements can facilitate discussions around cultural diversity, identity, and social justice issues. Therapists can incorporate videos, podcasts, or articles that highlight diverse perspectives and experiences, fostering empathy, understanding, and inclusivity in therapy sessions.

Multimedia resources can enhance the accessibility and flexibility of therapy sessions, particularly for clients with specific needs or constraints. For example, therapists may use online platforms for teletherapy sessions, provide audio recordings for clients with visual impairments, or offer subtitles for clients with hearing impairments.

Multimedia elements can aid memory and retention of therapeutic concepts and skills by providing visual and auditory cues that reinforce learning. Clients may recall and apply information more effectively when it is presented in multiple formats and modalities.

Incorporating multimedia elements can strengthen the therapeutic alliance between the client and therapist by demonstrating the therapist's commitment to innovation, creativity, and client-centered care. Clients may feel valued and supported when therapists integrate multimedia resources that cater to their unique needs and preferences.

Multimedia elements can inspire creative expression and exploration in therapy sessions. Therapists may encourage clients to create multimedia artifacts, such as digital collages, videos, or playlists, to represent their thoughts, feelings, and experiences, fostering self-expression and insight.

Just like Marcus, your clients benefit most when they're not just participants in an intensive but empowered travelers on a guided journey. The materials you create aren't just paper tools or digital supplements; they are bridges between insight and implementation. When thoughtfully designed, your workbooks, guides, and multimedia elements become extensions of your clinical presence, tools that deepen trust, clarify goals, and keep the work alive long after the session ends.

While this section has focused on optimizing your life as an intensive practitioner—from structure and scheduling to business systems and resource development—the true reward of that intentionality is seen in your clients' transformation. In the next section, we'll explore how to elevate client outcomes even further, starting with how to build safety and trust in the first five minutes, how to engage resistance with compassion, and how to empower clients, not just to heal, but to lead in their own growth.

PART 6

Elevating Client Outcomes

CHAPTER 21

Building Trust and Safety Fast

In a traditional therapy setting, the pace of building trust and connection is typically slower, since you meet with your client multiple times over a series of weeks or months, gradually getting to know your client over the course of time. Usually, in traditional therapy, the focus isn't as intense or immediate as in an intensive therapy setting. There isn't nearly as much pressure to build rapport quickly.

Even if you feel quite comfortable establishing rapport with your clients in a traditional setting, this chapter is an important one. Take into consideration the concentrated timeline and intensity of the subjects you and your client may be navigating together, and you'll begin to see why it's so important to establish rapport quickly.

Of course, many of your intensive clients will be clients that you've already seen in your practice, which makes building rapport simple... it already exists between you! You might recommend an intensive to your current clients if they need a deeper dive into a particular area of therapy, want to make accelerated progress (and are good candidates for it), need psychoeducation, or want to integrate others into their therapy (an individual who has been seeing you for their own work and now wants to incorporate their partner into their progress, for instance).

Establishing trust with existing clients in an intensive setting will likely come naturally to you.

With new clients, establishing trust quickly for an intensive takes a different approach.

Why Establishing Trust Quickly Is Important

In an intensive therapeutic setting, you and your client both want to maximize the effectiveness of therapy, address urgent needs, and improve their well-being and safety, all within a much more concentrated amount of time. To do this, you need to keep these five factors in mind:

Limited Time: Establishing trust and connection quickly allows you to make the most of the limited time available during the intensive and to facilitate meaningful progress in that short period.

Urgent Needs: Clients in intensive settings are often dealing with acute issues, crises, or high levels of distress. They require immediate support and intervention. Building trust and connection quickly enables you to address these urgent needs effectively and provide timely assistance.

Client Vulnerability: Clients in intensive settings may feel particularly vulnerable due to the urgency or severity of their situation. They need to feel safe, understood, and supported as they navigate their challenges. Building trust and connection quickly helps create a secure therapeutic environment where clients feel comfortable expressing themselves and seeking help.

Engagement and Motivation: Trust and connection are foundational for client engagement and motivation in therapy. When clients feel connected to their mental health professional and believe that they are understood and respected, they are more likely to actively participate in the therapeutic process and remain motivated to work towards their goals.

Risk Management: In some intensive settings, there may be heightened risk factors, such as suicidal ideation, self-harm, or violence. Establishing trust and connection quickly enables the practitioner to assess and manage these risks more effectively, as clients are more likely to disclose sensitive information and collaborate on safety planning when they trust their practitioner.

Steps to Establish Trust and Connection Quickly

The best time to start the rapport building process is during your screening call. You've likely drafted a screening call based on the work we've done together earlier in this book. Those steps covered *what* you need to do during a screening session, but building rapport is all about *how* you conduct the call. It is the "bedside manners" of your screening session.

Whether you conduct your screening session over the phone or via video call, these tips will help you and your client connect quickly, even before they are officially your client:

Warm Greeting: Start the call with a warm and friendly greeting. A client can tell right away if you're just phoning it in, so use a welcoming tone of voice to put the client at ease right from the beginning.

Active Listening: Listen attentively to the client's concerns, questions, and responses. Demonstrate that you are fully engaged by using verbal cues such as "I see" or "That's understandable," and nonverbal cues like nodding (if you're on a video call, that is). This can be more difficult than it sounds, especially if you've been conducting the same screening call over and over again for months. Remember, this is their first engagement with you and with intensive therapy. Do your best to make your script sound as little like a script as possible.

Empathy and Understanding: Show empathy towards the client's situation and concerns. Acknowledge their emotions and validate their experiences.

Clarity and Transparency: Be transparent about the purpose of the call, the screening process, and what the client can expect moving forward. This helps alleviate any anxiety or uncertainty the client may have.

Tailored Approach: Leave space in your script to personalize your communication based on the client's preferences, communication style, and cultural background. Adapt your language and tone to match theirs, and be respectful of any cultural sensitivities.

Building Trust: You can foster trust by being honest, genuine, and reliable. Follow through on any commitments made during the call, which will help undergird your professionalism and expertise.

Positivity and Optimism: Maintain a positive and optimistic attitude throughout the call, even when discussing challenging topics. Offer encouragement and reassurance to the client to instill confidence in the therapeutic process.

Respectful Inquiry: Ask open-ended questions to encourage the client to share their thoughts and feelings more freely. Respect their autonomy and avoid making assumptions or judgments. Again, this can be more challenging than it seems, especially if you've been "at it" for a while. Remember that every person is unique, every person has a story, and every story deserves your sincere and undivided attention.

Patience and Flexibility: Be patient and flexible, especially if the client is hesitant or unsure. Give them time to express themselves fully and provide reassurance as needed.

Closing on a Positive Note: End the call on a positive and encouraging note, even if you ultimately determine that an intensive is not the right path for them. Express gratitude for the client's time and willingness to engage, and reiterate your commitment to supporting them through the next steps. If you don't plan to accept their application, be prepared to offer them alternatives to your therapy so they feel empowered to take the next step for help.

Having a good screening script is absolutely essential for success in this area. Now is a good time to pull out your screening script draft and check it against these rapport-building tips. You might also ask a fellow practitioner or friend to listen to your script on the phone to see how it comes across to someone else. Practice your script several times before you connect with your prospective client as well.

The Psychology of Screening and Applications

Another important component to building rapport has to do with the difference between "signing up" for an intensive and "applying" to be admitted to an intensive. An application changes the connectivity and trust dynamics between the client and the practitioner even before the screening call. It also creates a sense of acceptance and qualification. These are important considerations in how you want to present your intensives.

When a client goes through the process of filling out an application, it often requires them to invest time and effort. This initial investment can create a sense of commitment to the process and a feeling of ownership over their decision to seek help. As a result, they may be more motivated to engage actively and honestly during screening calls or subsequent sessions, leading to stronger rapport.

Completing an application can be empowering for clients as it allows them to articulate their concerns, goals, and preferences in their own words. When practitioners review and acknowledge this information during screening or admission, it validates the client's experiences and feelings. This validation fosters a sense of trust and understanding, laying the groundwork for a strong therapeutic alliance.

A well-designed and thorough application process can signal to clients that the program or service is of high quality and credibility. This perception can positively influence their trust and confidence in the practitioners or organization behind it, making them more receptive to building rapport and connection during subsequent interactions.

The application process often serves as a form of screening to ensure that clients are a good fit for the program or service being offered. This selective process can enhance the perceived value of the service and contribute to a sense of exclusivity or belonging among those who are admitted. Clients who successfully complete the application process may feel a sense of accomplishment and pride, which can strengthen their commitment to the therapeutic process.

You should screen clients even for group-based intensives and recognize that there will be clients that you don't accept. In fact, your intensive's success depends on your selectiveness. The better you screen, the better they will go, the more successful your clients will be, and the more confident you will become as a specialized intensive practitioner.

All of this contributes to your client's perception of your practice and you as a practitioner, even before they arrive for your intensive. The successful screening and pre-intensive onboarding process should do the heavy lifting for rapport-building so that, when your client arrives, you'll be ready to hit the ground running.

Sustaining Rapport at the Intensive

You will of course reinforce the work that you've done in screening and onboarding when your client arrives for the intensive. Here are some basic tips that can help your client feel at ease and connected to you when they first arrive:

Give a Warm Welcome: Begin the session with a warm and welcoming greeting. Use the client's name, maintain eye contact, and offer a genuine smile to convey warmth and openness.

Recap Previous Interactions: Take a moment to recap the screening and application process, especially any particular details of their story that can make them feel heard and remembered.

Validate Their Journey: This is a significant investment of time and resources into their mental health, so take a moment to celebrate their journey in seeking help and acknowledge any challenges or barriers they may have faced along the way. Validate their courage and commitment to their own well-being.

Reiterate Goals and Expectations: Review the goals and expectations discussed during the screening process and clarify any misunderstandings. This reaffirms the collaborative nature of the therapeutic relationship and sets a clear direction for the session.

Express Commitment and Support: Reassure the client of your commitment to supporting them throughout the therapy process. Let them know that you are there to listen, understand, and assist them in reaching their goals.

Check In Emotionally: Take a moment to check in emotionally with the client. Ask how they are feeling at the beginning of the session and invite them to share any thoughts or concerns they may have.

Set the Tone: Set a positive and supportive tone for the session by expressing optimism about the client's progress and highlighting their strengths and resilience.

Re-establish Connection: Use active listening and empathy to re-establish the connection with the client. Reflect back on previous conversations, validate their experiences, and demonstrate understanding of their perspective.

Normalize Any Anxiety or Apprehension: If the client expresses any anxiety or apprehension about the session, normalize their feelings and reassure them that it's okay to feel nervous. Offer encouragement and support to help alleviate their concerns.

Review Confidentiality and Boundaries: Remind the client of the confidentiality of the therapeutic relationship and discuss any boundaries or limitations that may apply. This reinforces trust and helps them feel safe and secure.

Even if you've succeeded at building rapport and establishing trust through your screening and application process, there will be times during your intensives when your client feels resistant or ambivalent about this experience. In the next chapter, we'll go over how to recognize signs that your client is disengaging, ways to alleviate their hesitations, and tips to break through to your client when they begin to feel overwhelmed, stressed, or triggered.

CHAPTER 22

Engaging Resistance and Ambivalence

In the last chapter, we talked about how intentional practitioners need to be to build rapport with their clients, both prior to and during intensives. But even when a client fully trusts you and has complete confidence in your leadership through this process, a client can still feel resistant to or nervous about participating in sessions.

In this chapter, we'll look at what you can do to allay the fears and doubts of your clients before and during the intensive so their experience leads them into greater healing and recovery.

First, let's take a moment to get into the shoes of your potential clients to experience what it is that might be going on inside their minds.

Life Inside Your New Client's Mind

The day is finally here.

You listen to music and tap the steering wheel as you drive, doing your best to distract yourself from the nerves building up in your gut. You find a parking space and gather your things, feeling a little disoriented—did you remember your phone charger? Where are your keys?

Ah, they're in your hands.

As you approach the building where the intensive session will take place, your heart begins to race with anticipation and doubt. You've been wrestling with the decision to attend for weeks, torn between the hope of finding clarity, the fear of exposing your vulnerabilities, or even worse feelings of failure creeping in.

As you step inside the waiting area, your mind buzzes with questions. Can you really trust a stranger to unravel the complexities of your life in just three days? Will this intensive therapy be worth the hefty investment of your time and money? What if you open up about your deepest struggles and regrets, only to be met with judgment or indifference?

As the session begins and you settle into your chair, the doubts and fears only intensify. You find it difficult to focus as the mental health professional introduces themselves and outlines the agenda for the next three days. Your palms grow clammy, and your stomach churns with anxiety. What if you're not capable of making the changes necessary for healing? What if you become overwhelmed by the intensity of the emotions that surface? As the practitioner encourages you to share your story, you feel a knot forming in your throat. You want to speak up, to release the weight of your burdens, but the fear of being misunderstood or rejected holds you back. Each moment that passes feels like an eternity, your mind spinning with self-doubt and uncertainty.

Midway through the session, as the practitioner begins to delve deeper into your struggles, you feel a wave of panic rising within you. Your chest tightens, and your breathing becomes shallow and erratic. What if you're not ready to confront the pain buried deep within your psyche? What if you can't handle the emotional intensity of the therapeutic process?

As the anxiety threatens to overwhelm you, you struggle to maintain composure, desperately searching for an escape route from the vulnerability and discomfort. You question whether you have the strength and resilience to endure the challenges that lie ahead. The doubts and fears consume you, casting a shadow over the possibility of finding healing and renewal.

When to Address Your Client's Fears

These are real emotions, real questions, and real doubts that many of our clients will face at some point leading up to or during the intensive experience. It's important to understand this reality and design your intensive to address these fears.

You can begin this process as early as the first email communication. If you have a templated response to inquiries, make sure that it establishes both **empathy** and **credibility**. You have another opportunity to allay your client's fears during the screening process. Review your screening script to make sure that you've taken time to address how your potential client is feeling about the process.

All of the nerves they've been able to push into the background are likely to surface just as they arrive at your intensive, so look for ways to affirm your client and address their fears first thing at the beginning of your intensive, in the orientation process. Keep watch for signs of dysregulation throughout the intensive, and affirm your clients at the end of the intensive, when you are promoting aftercare.

Signs of Dysregulation

You will use the same skills you would in a traditional setting to help clients regulate, but keep in mind that some people experience hyperarousal and other people hypoarousal.

Signs of Hyperarousal Include:	Signs of Hypoarousal Include:
• Increased Heart Rate • Rapid Breathing • Muscle Tension • Heightened Sensitivity • Racing Thoughts • Irritability and Agitation • Difficulty Relaxing • Hypervigilance • Impulsivity • Physical Symptoms, like Sweating, Trembling, Dizziness, Gastrointestinal Distress, or Headaches	• Fatigue or Low Energy • Reduced Heart Rate • Shallow Breathing • Muscle Weakness • Numbness or Dissociation • Reduced Sensitivity • Difficulty Concentrating • Slowed Reaction Time • Reduced Emotional Responsiveness • Social Withdrawal • Avoidance Behavior • Difficulty Staying Awake

In an intensive setting, it's important to be able to recognize your client's attachment style quickly so that you can determine the best ways to make them feel safe.

Therapeutic Techniques to Address Trauma Responses

There are several different ways you can address your client's trauma responses:[35]

- Psychoeducation
- Grounding Techniques
- Safety Planning
- Trauma-Informed Mindfulness
- Somatic Experiencing
- Internal Family Systems (IFS)
- Trauma Narrative
- Resourcing
- Trauma-Focused Cognitive-Behavioral Therapy (TF-CBT)
- Attachment-Based Interventions

Use the techniques that you feel best suit your style and your client's needs, prioritizing their safety, stabilization, and empowerment. And of course, as always, make sure you feel properly trained for these techniques. We hope learning about new techniques will pique your interest, but we also want you to feel comfortable and confident as you step into new areas of expertise. We all have to start somewhere!

One last note, if you find yourself in an intensive with a reporting situation, give it the same attention you would in a traditional setting; however, you need to have a plan in place to handle the situation as a part of the intensive process. This includes knowing the mandatory reporting laws in your state, having a clear protocol for pausing the session if necessary, and informing the client in advance—preferably during your intake or consent process—about your reporting obligations. It's also wise to have contact information for local authorities or child protective services readily available, and to identify a confidential space where you can make required calls without disrupting the emotional flow of the intensive. Being prepared allows you to respond ethically and calmly while preserving as much trust and safety in the room as possible.

---

35 A more detailed explanation of Dysregulation and Trauma Response Therapy Tools is included in The Intensive Method online course and is available for download at theintensivemethod.com.

You're likely already employing techniques and concepts to manage your client's dysregulation or resistance in your traditional setting, so bring those rock-star practitioner capabilities over to your intensive practice!

Responding to Life Inside Your New Client's Mind

Let's imagine the same moment from the beginning of this chapter, but this time, from the other side of the room.

You notice your client's hands trembling as they fumble with their bag, eyes darting from wall to floor to door. You gently greet them by name, offer a seat, and express how glad you are that they made it. You take your time, not rushing through introductions but instead anchoring the moment in warmth and presence.

You begin with a simple orientation, designed with intention: clear expectations, plenty of reassurance, and small, early wins that build trust. You pause to normalize the swirl of emotions that many clients feel, naming anxiety, fear, and skepticism not as signs of failure, but as signs of courage. You let your client know that this space is theirs too, that your role is not to fix them, but to walk with them.

As the first session unfolds and you sense shallow breathing, hesitant speech, or zoning out, you make space. You slow things down. You name what you see without judgment. You offer a grounding exercise or a quick break. You remind them that they're not alone, that you've seen people step into hard truths and come out stronger, and that their pace is honored here.

You watch for dysregulation—not as a disruption, but as data. You adapt. You integrate touchpoints that reflect their attachment style, using steady presence, eye contact, or brief distance as needed. You choose interventions that are trauma-informed and attuned, always returning to safety and collaboration.

As you prepare for aftercare on the last day of the intensive, you affirm not only the work done but the strength it took to show up. You highlight progress, name resilience, and leave them with a tangible next step. You don't gloss over what was hard, but you make sure they leave with a sense of dignity and direction.

By the end of the intensive, the same client who once walked through the door with darting eyes, trembling hands, and a knot of fear in their chest now sits a little taller—shoulders less hunched, breathing deeper, their gaze steadier. The weight they carried is not gone, but it's been named, explored, and shared, and in that process, it's become lighter. Their face, once tense with anxiety, now holds a softness, maybe even a quiet confidence. There's a sense of clarity where there was once confusion. While the path ahead may still be challenging, they leave with tools in their hands, hope in their heart, and a renewed sense of agency.

They arrived unsure if healing was possible; they leave knowing they are already in motion, heading toward a brighter future.

This is what it means to lead with compassion and structure in an intensive. When clinicians prepare thoughtfully and respond relationally, even the most vulnerable beginning can lead to deep, life-changing work. In the next section, we'll shift our focus to how we can continue elevating client outcomes. In other words, in this chapter, we talked about moving your clients away from their fears. In the next chapter, we will cover moving your clients toward their goals.

CHAPTER 23

Empowering Clients As Collaborators

In the last chapter, we explored how resistance and ambivalence aren't obstacles to work around, they're invitations into deeper understanding. Now, we turn toward the posture that allows that understanding to grow: collaboration.

Empowering your client as a collaborator is more than a technique, it's a fundamental shift in how we hold space. Rather than assuming the role of expert with all the answers, the collaborative practitioner invites the client to take a seat at the table as a co-author of the process. This doesn't mean stepping back from your clinical role or expertise; instead, it means recognizing that transformation is most powerful when the client's voice, insight, and intuition are activated alongside your own.

In an intensive setting, this collaboration must be both intentional and structured. As we just saw, clients often arrive with uncertainty, doubt, or fear—about themselves, the process, and what might unfold—but when we create a space where they feel heard, respected, and invited into ownership, something shifts. Their buy-in increases. Their self-awareness sharpens. The work becomes theirs—not something done to them, but something done *with* them.

This chapter will explore how to build that kind of partnership, starting with the language you use, the questions you ask, and the ways you frame goals and feedback. We'll take a look at collaboration in the beginning, middle, and end of an intensive, and how empowering clients in this way doesn't just improve outcomes, it builds dignity, agency, and lasting change.

Why Collaboration Matters

Collaborating with a client on setting goals and priorities for any counseling setting, let alone an intensive session, is important for several reasons.

Client-Centered Approach: Practitioners are most effective when they have tailored their services to the specific needs and goals of the client. By involving the client in goal-setting, you ensure that the session is focused on addressing their concerns and aspirations.

Empowerment: Collaborating with the client empowers them to take an active role in their own healing process. It fosters a sense of ownership and commitment to the healing journey, which can enhance motivation and engagement.

Clarity and Focus: Setting clear goals and priorities helps both the practitioner and the client stay focused during the session. It provides a roadmap for what needs to be addressed and allows for more efficient use of time and resources.

Alignment of Expectations: Collaborative goal-setting ensures that there is alignment between the client's expectations and the practitioner's approach. This reduces the likelihood of misunderstandings or dissatisfaction with the process.

Measurement of Progress: Clearly defined goals allow for the measurement of progress over time. This not only helps track the program's effectiveness but also provides a sense of achievement and momentum for the client.

Cultivation of Therapeutic Alliance: Collaborating on goals fosters a sense of partnership and trust between the client and practitioner, which is foundational to the therapeutic alliance. A strong alliance enhances effectiveness and promotes positive outcomes.

Practical Strategies for Client Collaboration

Just like there are a lot of opportunities throughout the process to reassure your clients and alleviate their fears, there are also plenty of points throughout their relationship with you to bolster their confidence and enhance the possibility for a successful outcome on the other side of their intensive. You can introduce goal setting **during your screening call** and **in a follow-up email** after your screening call. It's important to revisit goals again **after orientation** in your first session to set the focus for your time together. This is especially important if some time has passed since the screening call you had with them. You can make adjustments to goals **throughout the intensive** as well. **At the end of the intensive**, you will want to evaluate whether or not your client feels they were able to meet the goals they set with you for the intensive, and outline new goals with you for their **aftercare plan**.

Revisiting Your Screening Call Script

Now is a good time to pull out your screening call script to make sure that you've incorporated some open-ended questions to help your client begin thinking about their goals and dreams for their intensive. Here are a few questions that may help your client process their goals while also giving you greater insight into how to personalize their treatment plan:

What specifically intrigues you regarding an intensive option at this particular moment? This question invites the client to articulate their reasons for seeking your services and can help identify initial areas of concern or desired changes.

What would you like to achieve or accomplish through the intensive? This question encourages the client to think about their goals and aspirations for the therapeutic process. It helps clarify their expectations and desired outcomes.

Can you tell me about any specific challenges or obstacles you're facing in your life right now? By asking about challenges, the practitioner can gain insight into areas where the client may be struggling and identify potential areas for goal-setting and intervention.

How do you envision your life looking differently once you've made progress? This question prompts the client to visualize their desired future and can reveal their hopes and dreams for personal growth and change.

Are there any particular strengths or resources you bring to the table that you'd like to build on during your intensive? Acknowledging strengths and resources empowers the client and can provide a foundation for goal-setting and problem-solving.

What have been your past experiences with therapy or personal development efforts? What worked well for you in those experiences, and

what didn't? Understanding the client's past experiences with therapy helps tailor the approach to their preferences and needs. It also provides insights into effective strategies for them.

What would help you hope to achieve with an intensive that you may not have been able to achieve in traditional therapy? This question invites the client to reflect on their own criteria for measuring progress, which can guide goal-setting and evaluation of outcomes.

Intensive Confirmation Email

As part of your onboarding and pre-intensive paperwork, you might include an invitation for your client to articulate their goals. Be cognizant of HIPAA requirements and make sure that any information you collect from your client is kept in a secure system. These questions could be part of your confirmation email or a link to a survey for them to complete as part of your onboarding packet.[36]

It's especially helpful to offer your client the opportunity to put their thoughts into writing, building upon what they were able to share with you over the phone or video call. Asking questions in writing allows the client to delve deeper into their thoughts and provides a structured format for them to identify and articulate goals, perceived obstacles, and fears. It also gives you a written record that both you and your client can refer back to throughout the intensive process.

These four questions can provide you with enhanced insights into your client's personality, attachment style, and preferences so that you can design the most effective intensive:

What are three things you would like to accomplish at the intensive? This question helps set clear goals and expectations for the intensive. It allows the client to articulate their priorities and desired outcomes, providing direction for the process. Asking this question in writing encourages the client to reflect on their goals thoughtfully and express them clearly. It also creates a record that both the client and practitioner can refer back to throughout the journey.

---

36 *A basic email confirmation template with questions you can ask your client as follow-up to your screening call is included with The Intensive Method online course and is available for download at theintensivemethod.com.*

What do you perceive as the top reasons you haven't been able to achieve these goals? Understanding the barriers or challenges that have hindered progress toward their goals is essential for effective intensives. This question helps identify underlying issues that may need to be addressed during the intensive.

What is at least one thing you have tried to do that hasn't worked to overcome these challenges? Exploring past attempts to overcome challenges provides valuable information about what strategies have been ineffective for the client. It helps identify patterns and informs the practitioner about potential areas for intervention.

Share at least one of your fears going into the intensive about your future? Acknowledging and addressing fears is important for creating a safe and supportive therapeutic environment. This question helps uncover any anxieties or concerns the client may have about the intensive process or their future. Asking this question allows them to explore and process their emotions at their own pace, facilitating a deeper level of self-awareness and vulnerability.

Articulating Goals for the Intensive after the Orientation

Once your client is with you in person and you've handled all of the necessary orientation practicalities, it's important to ask your client during their first session with you to share their hopes, dreams, and goals for the intensive again.

Even if this was completed during your screening call and collected via the survey we just talked about, giving your client the opportunity to voice their goals again helps to solidify the direction you plan to head together. It's a great way to join with the client in their outlook for the intensive. It will also help your client get grounded, present, and on the same page for what they're about to take on with you.

Addressing the Pivot

Intensives might be weeks or even months after you conducted a screening, and despite how well defined, planned, and organized your onboarding process, sometimes your client's situation will have changed since they first connected with you. Your clients might need to pivot directions or add other important items to the agenda.

The best time for this to surface is during that first session.

If this happens, you can always share with your client that you need a little time to synthesize the new information into the plan for the rest of the intensive. Let them know that you would like to continue as planned for the first day or the morning session. You can always recalibrate your plans for the rest of the intensive over the lunch break or in the evening.

When Things Go Sideways

Clients can and will throw curve balls from time to time. Remember, *you are in control, not the client.* As a practitioner, you want to be confident and flexible but also in control and regulated.

If a client brings something that is either inappropriate or out of bounds of your scope, or you find yourself dysregulated, do what you need to do to take care of yourself. Don't be afraid to take a break. Establish and hold boundaries with your client. Be assertive.

Worst-case scenario, give clients the freedom to terminate the intensive if that is their choice and offer to either refund them their money or bank the fees paid toward future care.

These scenarios can happen, but the vast majority of your experiences should go smoothly, especially if you have the appropriate steps in place to set expectations and collaborate with your client from the beginning. So don't worry, this is not the norm.

End-of-Intensive Goals

If you follow the structure for goal setting that we covered earlier, then you already have the framework for revisiting goals throughout each day of the intensive. At the end of your intensive, you will revisit your client's goals and develop an aftercare plan together. This usually takes place in the afternoon of Day 3.

Here are some recommendations for revisiting your client's goals at the end of the intensive:

Reflect on Progress: Begin by reflecting on the progress the client has made toward their initial goals during the intensive sessions. Highlight specific achievements and areas of growth.

Review Initial Goals: Review the goals that were set at the beginning of the intensive session. Discuss with the client whether these goals were achieved, partially achieved, or require further work.

Explore Client's Perspective: Ask your client about their experience during the intensive sessions. Explore how they feel about the progress they've made and whether their goals still resonate with them.

Identify Adjustments: If necessary, collaboratively identify any adjustments or refinements to the client's goals based on their evolving needs, insights gained during sessions, or changes in their circumstances.

Celebrate Achievements: Take the time to acknowledge and celebrate the client's achievements and progress, no matter how small. This validation reinforces their sense of accomplishment and motivates them for further growth.

Aftercare Plan Goal Setting

It's important to evaluate the goals your client set for the intensive, but they also need to go back to their real life. This is your chance to collaborate with your client and empower them to be successful. After you've gone over your client's goals and achievements from the last three days, it's time to look forward to life after the intensive.

Outlining New Goals for Aftercare Plan

Reflect on Intensive Experience: Reflect on the client's overall experience during the intensive sessions. Discuss what aspects of the sessions were most beneficial and how they can continue to build on these strengths in their aftercare plan.

Identify Areas for Continued Growth: Collaboratively identify areas in which the client would like to continue working on or developing after the intensive concludes. This may include building coping skills, improving relationships, or addressing specific challenges.

Set SMARTER Goals: Help the client set new goals for their aftercare plan that are Specific, Measurable, Achievable, Relevant, and Time-bound (SMART). Ensure that these goals are aligned with their values, priorities, and long-term aspirations. Pro Tip: You can add E and R to SMART Goals for clients at aftercare: E - stands for Evaluate, and R stands for Reward or Revise!

Develop Action Steps: Break down each goal into actionable steps that the client can take to work towards achieving them. Discuss potential obstacles and strategies for overcoming them.

Create Supportive Environment: Explore ways to create a supportive environment for the client to continue their progress. This may involve connecting them with resources, recommending self-care practices, or involving their support network.

Establish Follow-Up Plan: Determine how and when the client will follow up with their progress on their aftercare goals. Schedule regular check-ins or appointments to monitor their progress, provide support, and make adjustments as needed.

By revisiting the client's goals at the end of the intensive and outlining new goals for their aftercare plan, you are able to reinforce the client's agency and commitment to their continued growth and well-being.

At the heart of intensive work is the belief that healing happens best *with* clients, not *for* them. When we treat clients as collaborators—inviting their insight, honoring their agency, and sharing the weight of the work—we cultivate trust, increase engagement, and foster deeper, more lasting change. Collaboration doesn't mean letting go of our role as guide; it means guiding in a way that draws out the client's wisdom, strength, and ownership. In doing so, we empower them not only to participate in their healing but to carry it forward, long after the intensive ends.

Clearly, transformation doesn't end when the intensive does. The most powerful breakthroughs are sustained by what happens next. We'll turn to aftercare programs in the next chapter.

CHAPTER 24

Rigorous Aftercare and Sustained Success

At this point in your reading, you probably have a solid structure for your daily schedule during an intensive. As a reminder, we recommend checking in with your client to review their progress on a regular basis throughout the intensive. This includes a feelings check at the start of every session and another check-in at the end of every day, during which the client should be encouraged to share highlights of that day's learning, any "aha" moments they experienced, things that challenged them, and areas that need more exploration.

Lastly, it's important to check in with your client again at the end of the intensive.

Setting Up the Aftercare Plan

We've talked about the importance of goal setting with your client for their aftercare plan, but what options are available for your client within your own practice? We highly recommend designing some form of an aftercare plan.

Aftercare sessions are important for your client for a number of reasons:

Transitioning Back to Everyday Life: Intensive therapy sessions can be emotionally and mentally taxing. Aftercare sessions provide a structured transition back into the client's regular routine by offering support and guidance as they reintegrate into their daily life.

Continuation of Progress: Therapy doesn't end after the intensive session. Aftercare sessions allow the client to continue working on the goals and insights gained during the intensive. This ensures that the progress made during the intensive session is sustained and built upon.

Addressing Emerging Issues: Sometimes, new issues or challenges may arise after the intensive session. Aftercare sessions provide an opportunity for the client to address these emerging issues in a supportive environment, preventing them from derailing progress.

Reinforcement and Accountability: Aftercare sessions reinforce the strategies, coping mechanisms, and insights learned during the intensive. They also provide a level of accountability, encouraging the client to implement these tools in their daily life.

Preventing Relapse: Intensive therapy sessions can bring about significant breakthroughs, but relapses are also a possibility for those who may be in recovery or if new crisis situations arise. Aftercare sessions help minimize the risk of relapse by providing ongoing support, monitoring, and intervention when necessary.

Building a Support Network: Aftercare sessions can involve group therapy or support groups, allowing clients to connect with others who have undergone similar experiences. This sense of community can be invaluable in maintaining motivation and resilience.

It's up to you to determine the timing and structure of aftercare sessions. We generally hold the first day-long aftercare session three months after the intensive. After that, our clients come back for aftercare at six-month intervals for 18-36 months, depending on their progress. We set up that expectation with our clients from the onset with our initial screening call, then reinforce it often throughout the 3-day intensive, solidifying the appointment at the end of the intensive so they have a clear understanding of the importance of aftercare and how many aftercare sessions they should expect to attend in the future.

You could schedule your sessions a week or two after the intensive or as far out as several months. It all depends upon the client, the goals you've set together, and of course your own schedule. You want to give your client time and space to process their experience but also strike a balance. If too much time lapses between sessions, a client might grow discouraged or be more likely to relapse or not return.

We recommend holding aftercare sessions in-person, but teletherapy may be an option depending on your state's and their state's regulations. Clients tend to understand the need for an in-person aftercare session, but it's helpful to reinforce the purpose of these sessions.

Other Ways to Support Your Client's Recovery after Intensives

In addition to day-long aftercare sessions with your clients, there are additional strategies you can recommend for your client's aftercare plan. We recommend at least one day of aftercare, but you might recommend more days spaced out over a series of months, or an additional day of specialized care, like Trauma Work with EMDR, for example, in addition to your standard aftercare appointment. You can also recommend other intensives that you offer with a different focus. We have a sequence of intensives that build upon each other based on the phase of recovery a person is in, so a client who starts with a Foundations of Recovery Intensive could advance to the next intensive one year from now. Alternatively, you might recommend an intensive that will focus on a different area of their mental health and wellness. Perhaps during the intensive, you discover that the client would benefit from some more concentrated time focusing on Family of Origin, for instance. You might recommend to your client to participate in a group intensive or other group-based opportunities.

Scheduling and Shaping Your Aftercare Plan

Before the end of the intensive, you should book the aftercare day on your calendar and theirs, and if they have any interest in other options, give them the opportunity to sign up for those as well.

You'll want to revisit your business systems to make sure you have a plan for receiving their deposit, whether that's an in-person transaction onsite or in a follow-up email. Regardless of the method of deposit, you'll want to send an email confirmation for the next aftercare session as well as any specific instructions for aftercare and an email evaluation of the intensive.

Take some time to reflect on your particular area of practice to develop a starting point for your aftercare plan. You might choose to draft a comprehensive aftercare plan to serve as your template. Then, when it's time to set goals for aftercare with your client, you can make a copy of your template and delete any bullets that don't pertain to your client's personal treatment plan.[37]

---

37 *The Intensive Method online course includes journaling exercises to help you generate ideas for aftercare, and a client aftercare treatment plan template is available through the course and for download at theintensivemethod.com.*

Your Client's Achievements and Next Steps

By the end of the intensive, your client should feel simultaneously exhausted and inspired. They've been through the mental health ringer, but all of that wringing out should leave them feeling lighter and more hopeful rather than beaten down and defeated. Your goal, at the end of the intensive, is to end your time together on the highest notes possible and send your client back into the world prepared to continue their journey of growth and healing.

To do this, you want to celebrate what they've accomplished during their time with you. Congratulate your client on their hard work. We give medallions to our clients to commemorate the three days they've spent with us. Encourage them in specific ways about their upcoming goals and objectives, which you've already outlined with them earlier in the day. Affirm them for who they are as a person and be sure to share how highly you regard their trust in you to do this work with them, and what a privilege it is for you as a practitioner to share in such important work on their journey.

The way you end your intensives lends itself to the future success and growth of your practice. In the next chapter, we'll go over strategies for evaluating your intensives and collecting client feedback.

CHAPTER 25

Client and Clinician Evaluation Tools

Evaluating your intensive is not just a professional best practice—it's essential to its long-term success. Without regular assessment, even the most well-designed intensive can stagnate, miss its mark, or fail to evolve with your clients' needs. Thoughtful evaluation allows you to measure outcomes, refine your approach, and ensure that both the clinical impact and business sustainability of your intensive remain strong. It's how you stay aligned with your mission, deliver consistently excellent care, and position your practice for continued growth and transformation.

Feedback provides valuable insights into the effectiveness of the intensive therapy program. Understanding what worked well and what didn't can help you refine your methods and improve the overall quality of care you deliver during an intensive.

Asking your clients for feedback shows them that their opinions and experiences are valued, which can increase satisfaction with the therapy process. Feeling heard and understood fosters a sense of trust and rapport between the client and practitioner. Understanding how your clients experienced the intensive and what they preferred can help you tailor future interventions for them, whether they continue in an aftercare plan or return for an additional intensive later on.

Feedback also provides a means of evaluating your client's progress and outcomes following the intensive. Most likely, your client will submit their feedback days after the experience, which will provide you insight into what the client retained from the experience, helping you gauge effectiveness.

Actively seeking feedback demonstrates your continued commitment to transparency and improvement, which can strengthen the therapeutic alliance between you and your clients. Trust is foundational in therapy, and feedback can help solidify that trust.

Your program evaluations are also a great place to gather client endorsements and reviews. Make sure that your evaluation includes a checkbox that allows your client to opt-out of sharing their feedback, and note how it might be used (for instance, you might ask your client for permission to use portions of their feedback as promotional content on your website but only cite their first name and last initial, or initials only plus their city and state, or something like that to protect their identities).

Let's talk about some of the practical steps and opportunities for soliciting feedback from your clients.

Intensive Evaluation Forms

The best time to request client feedback is immediately after an intensive has ended. This can be part of your follow-up communication regarding their aftercare plan or a separate email entirely—it's up to you. Keeping the two subjects separate may be beneficial to make sure that your evaluation doesn't get lost in the details of their aftercare plan.[38]

I highly recommend using a digital survey system so that you have an easy way to collect and analyze data down the road. When you set up your evaluation form, keep in mind the outcomes you want to achieve and not just what would be nice to know. Good data in translates into good data out. I recommend including sliding scale questions with several different weighted options (from very satisfied to completely unsatisfied, for example) as well as open-ended questions to collect their additional thoughts. A variety of questions will provide you with both quantitative and qualitative data to process later on.

Here are some key components of a qualitative and quantitative evaluation tool to consider incorporating into your feedback forms:

---

38 Sample emails and evaluation forms are included in The Intensive Method online course and can be downloaded from theintensivemethod.com.

- **Overall Experience:** Ask clients to provide feedback on their overall experience during the 3-day intensive therapy. This could include their impressions of the program structure, organization, and environment.
- **Effectiveness of Interventions:** Inquire about the effectiveness of specific therapeutic interventions used during the intensive. Clients can provide feedback on which techniques or approaches were helpful and which ones may not have resonated with them.
- **Quality of Therapeutic Relationship:** Explore clients' perceptions of the therapeutic relationship formed during the intensive. Ask about their comfort level, trust in the practitioner, and whether they felt heard and understood.
- **Emotional Safety:** Assess the extent to which clients felt emotionally safe and supported during the intensive. This includes asking about any concerns or areas where they may have felt vulnerable or uncomfortable.
- **Progress and Insights:** Encourage clients to reflect on any progress or insights gained during the 3-day intensive. Explore what they learned about themselves, their behaviors, and their coping mechanisms.
- **Logistical Feedback:** Gather feedback on logistical aspects of the program, such as scheduling, accommodations, meals, and any other practical considerations. This helps identify areas for improvement in the overall experience.
- **Suggestions for Improvement:** Invite clients to offer suggestions for how the intensive program could be enhanced or improved in the future. This could include ideas for additional activities, topics to explore, or adjustments to the format.
- **Follow-Up Support Needs:** Discuss clients' ongoing support needs following the intensive experience. Explore whether they feel adequately equipped to continue their therapeutic journey and identify any additional resources or support systems they may require.

Client Progress Reports

There are two different kinds of feedback forms I recommend setting up: one that is customized for each intensive that you offer, and a second feedback form that can serve as an ongoing progress report with your clients. An established feedback loop continually reinforces all of the trust building and quality improvement objectives a good practitioner wants to maintain.

Depending on the aftercare plan for your client, the regular feedback form, or Progress Report, could be sent weekly, monthly, or quarterly, containing the same basic content each time.[39]

You might confidentially collect HIPAA-compliant information about your client's goals and objectives as well as any relevant updates they want to send to you to help you adjust their treatment plan. The Progress Report feedback form ought to be shared with your client as regularly as you meet with them, but your client doesn't have to complete that form every time either. If they don't have anything new to share with you, then they might opt out of completing it.

You might decide to send this type of form only when you feel as if your client's progress is stalling, in order to solicit additional information from them about their progress, which can help you determine the best next step.

The ultimate goal in all of these efforts is to encourage the client to engage as fully as possible with the therapeutic process.

You might ask the following questions on your client feedback form:

1. **What is one thing you highly value regarding our working relationship? Why?**
2. **What is one thing that challenges you in our working relationship that you would like to address or change? Why?**
3. **Would you please provide any general feedback for consideration?**
4. **Do you have any potential solutions for consideration?**

Analyzing Evaluation Data for Insights

You just received your very first evaluation feedback from your very first intensive. Fantastic! Getting these forms isn't always easy. Here are a few do's and don'ts to help you analyze the feedback you receive.

---

39 A client feedback form template is included in The Intensive Method online course and can be downloaded from theintensivemethod.com.

Do's:

- **Maintain Objectivity:** Approach the data analysis process with an open mind and avoid bias. Especially after your first few intensives, you might feel defensive of the program you've put together, but try to focus on the facts presented in the data rather than your preconceived notions or expectations.
- **Look for Patterns and Trends:** Identify recurring themes or patterns in the data that may indicate areas of strength or areas needing improvement in therapy interventions. In order to do this, it's important to wait until you have a pool of responses before you start to make any massive changes to your program.
- **Compare Data over Time:** Track changes in evaluation data over time to assess progress and identify any emerging trends or patterns. This longitudinal analysis can provide valuable information about the effectiveness of interventions.
- **Collaborate with Colleagues:** You've invested a lot of time, energy, and heart into planning this intensive, which can make it difficult to see any critical feedback objectively. Consider discussing evaluation data with colleagues or peers in the industry to gain different perspectives and insights. Collaborative analysis can lead to more comprehensive understandings of the data and potential strategies for improvement.
- **Use Data to Inform Your Practice:** If you've set up your evaluations correctly, you should be able to draw some quantitative conclusions that you can then translate into actionable steps for improving your practice. Utilize data-driven decision-making to refine interventions, adjust treatment plans, or implement new strategies.
- **Communicate Findings Effectively:** Clearly communicate the findings of the data analysis to relevant stakeholders, including colleagues in your office and relevant supporting personnel, especially those who have a hand in shaping future endeavors. Reading through evaluations from clients can help all staff members understand how their role impacts the client experience and can help them make any adjustments they need to make on their end.

Here are a few things you should *not* do:

Don'ts:

- **Dismiss Negative Feedback:** It's so tempting to write-off negative feedback as clients just being out of touch or not understanding the therapeutic process! Do your best to avoid dismissing negative feedback or criticism from evaluation data. Instead, reframe this or view it as an opportunity for growth and improvement.
- **Rely Solely on Quantitative Data:** While quantitative data can provide valuable insights, don't overlook the qualitative aspects of evaluation data. Qualitative feedback and client narratives can offer rich contextual information that complements quantitative findings. Be sure that whatever evaluation forms you create include space for open-ended responses.
- **Ignore Outliers:** Pay attention to outliers in the data, as they may contain valuable information or indicate areas of particular significance. Investigate the reasons behind outliers rather than dismissing them.
- **Overlook Client Preferences:** Consider clients' preferences and individual differences when interpreting evaluation data. You've delivered a customized intensive experience for each of your clients, so you probably should expect your clients to respond differently as well. What works well for one client may not work for another, so avoid applying a one-size-fits-all approach.
- **Make Assumptions:** Refrain from making assumptions or jumping to conclusions based on limited data. If it's the first evaluation you've received and they've bashed everything about the experience, maybe take a breath, take a step back, and wait to make drastic changes based on their feedback. Instead, take the time to thoroughly analyze the data, gather additional responses from your next intensive, and consider multiple perspectives before drawing conclusions.
- **Neglect Professional Development:** Don't overlook opportunities for professional development based on evaluation data findings. Use insights gained from data analysis to identify areas for further training or skill development.

- **Lose Sight of Ethical Considerations:** Maintain confidentiality and uphold ethical standards when analyzing evaluation data. Ensure that data is handled and interpreted in accordance with professional guidelines and regulations.
- **Stop Offering Intensives or Avoid Moving Forward:** If you receive negative feedback, don't let imposter syndrome or rejection sensitivity keep you from continuing in your practice. Seek support from colleagues or your own therapy, especially if you're battling imposter syndrome in other aspects of your practice. We don't want you to feel frozen by negative feedback. We want you to be able to utilize it and move forward in a more successful way.

How to Make Strategic Changes to Your Intensives

Once you've gathered feedback from your clients, there are many ways you could use that feedback to improve your intensive therapy services. You don't want that feedback to just sit on a shelf.

If you plan to iterate on service offerings, you might consider implementing small-scale pilots of new or modified services based on feedback before a full rollout. Be open to making changes in response to feedback, even if they require significant shifts. Your practice will benefit from regularly updating and refining your services based on ongoing feedback and market trends.

It might be that client feedback prompts opportunities for you to consider revising your pricing structures. This could mean lowering or increasing your price. Adjust pricing based on the perceived value to the client rather than just costs. You could also consider offering different service tiers to cater to various client budgets and needs as long as it's within your regulations.

In addition to your evaluation feedback, make sure you regularly compare your pricing with competitors to ensure you remain competitive.

Your client feedback can help you refine your marketing strategies. Use client feedback to understand different client segments and tailor marketing messages accordingly. Create content that addresses common client concerns and highlights how your services meet their needs. And of course, use positive feedback and testimonials in your marketing materials to build trust and credibility.

When you're developing your evaluation tools, be sure to define key performance indicators (KPIs) related to client satisfaction, service usage, and revenue growth to track the impact of any changes you make.

By systematically collecting, analyzing, and acting on feedback, and staying attuned to market dynamics, you can continuously optimize your service offerings, delivery methods, pricing structures, and marketing strategies to enhance client satisfaction and drive revenue growth.

At this point, we've covered everything you need to know to launch an intensive effectively—how to structure it, serve your clients well, and sustain the model for long-term success. You have the tools, the framework, and the vision. So what's holding you back?

For many clinicians, the barrier isn't strategy—it's self-doubt. Questions creep in: *Am I really ready for this? Do I know enough? What if I fail?* These aren't just passing thoughts; they're the internal resistance that can quietly sabotage your next step. In the next chapter, we're going to confront one of the most common—and limiting—obstacles to growth: imposter syndrome. We'll explore how to recognize it, reframe it, and move forward with the confidence that you are more ready than you think.

CHAPTER 26

Taking the Leap: Mindset Shifts for Clinicians

At this point in your exploration of The Intensive Method, you may be encountering some internal barriers many practitioners face when transitioning to this specialized approach.

Embracing The Intensive Method requires not just a shift in technique, but a shift in mindset. Imposter syndrome is a common experience among practitioners venturing into intensives. It's that nagging feeling of self-doubt and inadequacy, despite your qualifications and accomplishments. You might find yourself thinking:

"Am I really capable of delivering such impactful therapy?"

"What if I don't have what it takes to handle intensive sessions?"

"Other practitioners seem so much more skilled and experienced than me."

These thoughts can be paralyzing, but remember, they are a normal part of growth. We all experience these feelings from time to time. Recognizing the thought patterns that can hinder your progress along this journey is the first step towards overcoming them.

Common thought patterns that can trigger imposter syndrome include perfectionism, comparison, and fear of failure.

Perfectionism involves setting exceedingly high standards for yourself. It can lead to excessive self-criticism and a fear of making mistakes. Perfectionism can cause paralysis by analysis, where you spend too much time planning and refining your offerings without ever launching them. This hesitation can delay your progress and undermine your confidence.

Comparison involves measuring your progress against others. This can lead to feelings of inadequacy and self-doubt. Constantly comparing yourself to others can erode your self-esteem and lead to a lack of motivation. It can also create unnecessary stress and distract you from focusing on your own unique strengths and journey.

The fear of failure involves an intense worry about not meeting expectations or making mistakes, which can prevent you from taking necessary risks. This fear can lead to avoidance behavior. You might procrastinate or shy away from starting this initiative. It can also result in a lack of creativity, stifling your potential to innovate and grow your practice.

These thought patterns can lead to hesitation and a lack of confidence, preventing you from taking the leap into this rewarding area of practice.

Strategies for Reframing Self-Perception and Building Confidence

Friend, you don't have to be perfect. You are going to make mistakes. It's okay. Stop comparing yourself to other practitioners. You have what it takes to meet the demands of intensives.

Of course, me saying these things to you isn't going to be enough to overcome imposter syndrome. This takes hard work on your part. To combat these self-doubts, consider these strategies:

Acknowledge Your Expertise: Reflect on your training, experiences, and successes. Recognize that you have a strong foundation to build upon. When you find yourself wrestling with "Do I have what it takes" kinds of thoughts, it might help to journal or dialogue with a trusted friend about your personal and professional journey. This can help instill in you the confidence robbed by imposter syndrome.

Embrace Continuous Learning: With a solid foundation of confidence about what it is you already know, allow humility to be your guide as well. Becoming proficient in intensives is a journey. If you stay humble, you make room for curiosity, and curiosity leads to even more growth. Embrace learning opportunities, outside consultative feedback, and peer support.

Reframe Failures as Learning Opportunities: We all fail from time to time. True success isn't achieved by perfection, but by perseverance, resilience, and hope. View mistakes not as failures, but as valuable lessons that contribute to your growth.

Practice Self-Compassion: Treat yourself with the same kindness and understanding you offer your clients. If you find yourself in a loop of negative self-talk, consider what you would tell a client if they were saying similar things—and then apply that same compassion to yourself.

Visualize Success: Imagine successful outcomes and the positive impact you'll have on your clients. Visualization can help build confidence and reduce anxiety.

Here's another way to think about the difference between what you traditionally offer your clients and The Intensive Method.

We all have memories of friendships formed throughout our school years, those people we met on the playground, through a sport, or in a group project. Your friendship began slowly and grew over time. Maybe one of you asked the other to play after school. You started to hang out more on the weekends. The more time you spent together, the more your friendship grew. Friendships formed this way are a lot like the relationships formed in traditional therapy sessions—they build steadily and make progress over time.

But if you ever went away as a kid for a week of summer camp, you already understand the power of intensives and different kinds of relationships that are possible in an intensive setting.

The immersive nature of summer camp as a kid allowed you to form deep, meaningful relationships in a very short period of time. Friendships formed at camp developed rapidly over a concentrated period by overcoming common challenges and sharing profound experiences. There are no other distractions at summer camp, and that intense, focused time spent together can lead to significant growth and breakthroughs in a very short period of time. For many kids, that one week of summer camp was a life changing experience.

That's the power of intensives. By offering our services through The Intensive Method, we're able to carve out the same space for deep, transformative experiences to happen for adults who are hurried, frenzied, and busy beyond all belief, incapable of taking even a few minutes out of their days to slow down and process what's happened to them, what's happening to them, and how they are responding to the events in their lives. Through intensives, we can invite them to step off the hamster wheel of their lives, collect their thoughts and emotions, and find healing for their hearts and minds.

We have a profound opportunity to make a difference for people who find themselves rattled, anxious, exhausted, traumatized, wounded, and trapped by the challenges they face everyday.

And you have what it takes to deliver that experience.

As you embark on this new path, remember that stepping into intensives is both a professional and personal evolution. It's an opportunity to profoundly impact your clients' lives, facilitating deep and meaningful change. The initial self-doubt and challenges are natural, but by reframing your mindset and embracing your journey, you can confidently take the leap.

There's so much for you as a practitioner here, as well. Traditional approaches to mental health care work for many people, but certainly we all feel the grind and exhaustion of being on that same hamster wheel many of our clients are on themselves. Intensives provide you with the opportunity to take a breath, invest in yourself, and lead a more free, fulfilling, and profitable practice. **Believe in your capabilities, embrace the challenges, and look forward to the remarkable growth and fulfillment that lies ahead.**

In taking this leap, you're not just enhancing your skills—you're expanding your capacity to make a significant difference. Welcome the journey with open arms, and remember, every step forward is a testament to your dedication and passion for helping others.

Parts 7 and 8 are designed to support practitioners who are looking for ways to further grow and expand their intensive practice, whether through diversifying their offerings or investing in leadership development. If you're at the initial stage of launching your intensive practice, you might read these chapters with a visionary mindset rather than an eye for immediate implementation. Allow yourself to dream a little about what the future of your practice could look like. Don't let the possibilities overwhelm you; instead, imagine the kind of life and career that intensives could provide. And then take the first right step to make it happen.

PART 7

Expand Your Intensive Revenue Streams

CHAPTER 27

Creating Intensive Therapy Products to Expand Revenue Streams

There are many other ways you can monetize your intensive therapy practice to further increase your revenue, beyond the foundational intensive. In this chapter, we'll explore supplemental products you can offer to support your clients while also benefiting your bottom line.

Having therapeutic products available for purchase before, during, or after an intensive therapy session can offer several benefits to clients:

Continuity of Care: Clients can continue their therapeutic journey beyond the intensive session by incorporating therapeutic products into their daily routines. This promotes continuity of care and supports ongoing progress between their intensive and future traditional therapy sessions or aftercare sessions.

Enhanced Self-Care Practices: Therapeutic products such as relaxation kits, stress relief tools, and sensory integration tools provide clients with tangible resources to support their self-care practices. These products empower clients to take an active role in managing their mental health and well-being.

Extended Support: Intensive therapy sessions can be emotionally and mentally taxing, and having therapeutic products available for purchase provides clients with extended support beyond the session. Clients can use these products to reinforce therapeutic techniques learned during the session and cope with challenges as they arise.

Customized Treatment Plans: Therapists can recommend specific therapeutic products based on clients' needs, preferences, and treatment goals. This allows for a customized approach to therapy that addresses clients' unique circumstances and promotes positive outcomes.

Increased Engagement and Motivation: Offering therapeutic products before, during, or after an intensive therapy session can increase clients' engagement and motivation in the therapeutic process. Having access to tangible resources reinforces the value of therapy and encourages clients to actively participate in their treatment.

Convenience and Accessibility: Therapeutic products provide clients with convenient and accessible tools to support their mental health and well-being. Clients can access these products at their own convenience, whether it's during therapy sessions, at home, or on the go.

Improved Coping Skills: Therapeutic products such as guided imagery recordings, journals, and relaxation tools can help clients develop and strengthen coping skills to manage stress, anxiety, and other challenges. These products offer practical strategies and techniques for navigating difficult emotions and situations.

Long-Term Benefits: By incorporating therapeutic products into their daily routines, clients can experience long-term benefits such as improved mood, reduced stress levels, enhanced self-awareness, and greater resilience. These benefits contribute to overall well-being and quality of life.

Overall, having therapeutic products available for purchase before, during, or after an intensive therapy session enhances the client's therapeutic experience, promotes self-care and empowerment, and supports long-term progress and well-being.

Perhaps you want to have some available for purchase in the office. You might send your clients affiliate links for others, or you could just simply resource your clients with information that lets them know they are available.

So, what types of products could work for your practice? First and foremost, you want to take into consideration the needs and preferences of your clients when thinking about products. Take some time to brainstorm what might be beneficial for your clients and make sure these products are evidence-based and aligned with therapeutic goals.[40]

---

40 *A guided journaling exercise for this is included in The Intensive Method online course.*

There are five different categories of therapeutic products that might work for your practice:

1. Therapeutic Tools for Stress Relief
2. Mindfulness and Relaxation Kits
3. Therapeutic Journals and Workbooks
4. Sensory Integration Tools
5. Guided Imagery and Visualization Resources

Therapeutic Tools for Stress Relief

In case you missed it, here it is again: intensive therapy can be intense for our clients. Your practice can offer clients tools to relieve their stress while they are in your office and when they return to their everyday lives.

You might consider offering one of the following tools to help relieve your clients' stress:

Stress Balls, some of which are infused with calming scents like lavender or chamomile.

Fidget Toys, which can be branded with your company logo.

Aromatherapy, including offering essential oils and diffusers to help create a calming environment while in the office and when they return home.

Massage Tools, such as handheld massagers, massage balls, or massage cushions to help relieve muscle tension and promote relaxation.

Nature Sounds, Guided Relaxation Tracks, or Music on CDs or MP3s (accessible through your website) can help individuals unwind and reduce their stress levels.

Coloring Books and Art Supplies to help your clients reduce stress and promote mindfulness. You might consider hiring an independent graphic designer or contracting someone from sites like Etsy or Upwork to custom design an adult coloring book for your practice.

Mindfulness and Relaxation Kits

In addition to individual therapeutic tools, you might consider developing a kit for your clients to enhance their practice. This kit could contain items such as a meditation cushion, essential oils, and a guided meditation CD; a journal, a pen, and a soothing candle; or perhaps a coloring book, art supplies, and a fidget spinner.

These kits are useful for clients, and clients might also see their value as gift sets for friends or loved ones, as well. You can make different types of kits or you can have them assemble their own kit by having multiple items available for them to choose from. This is a great opportunity to be creative!

Therapeutic Journals and Workbooks

Customized therapeutic journals and workbooks are another way you can enhance and differentiate your practice from other practitioners. A guided journal with prompts for self-reflection and emotional processing can be used to supplement sessions in the evening between days of the intensive, or you might have a similar guided journal available to help a client process and continue their work once they leave your intensive. Or both!

You can also create and order simple journals that have a custom-branded cover with blank journal pages inside that can be an attractive, useful product to offer your clients.

Sensory Integration Tools

Sensory integration tools are designed to provide sensory input and help individuals regulate their sensory experiences. These tools are commonly used by individuals with sensory processing difficulties, autism spectrum disorder, attention deficit hyperactivity disorder (ADHD), anxiety, and other sensory-related challenges.

If these tools are useful for your clients during the intensive, they may be interested in buying them to take home for their personal use.

Here are some examples of sensory integration tools you could offer your clients:

Weighted Blankets: These blankets are filled with evenly distributed weights, such as glass beads or pellets, providing deep pressure stimulation. They can help individuals feel grounded, calm anxiety, and promote relaxation.

Weighted Vests: Similar to weighted blankets, weighted vests provide deep pressure input to the body, promoting a sense of calm and reducing sensory overload. They can be worn discreetly under clothing and are often used in sensory integration therapy.

Compression Clothing: Compression clothing, such as compression shirts, vests, or socks, applies gentle pressure to the body, providing proprioceptive input and promoting body awareness. This can help individuals feel more grounded and focused.

Chewelry: These are wearable items designed for individuals who have a need to chew or bite as a way to regulate sensory input. Chewelry includes chewable necklaces, bracelets, and pencil toppers made of safe, non-toxic materials.

Fidget Toys: We talked about fidget toys as a possible therapeutic tool for stress relief, but these tools are also handy objects that can provide sensory stimulation and promote focus. Some examples include fidget spinners, stress balls, tangles, and textured sensory stones.

Sensory Brushes: Sensory brushes, also known as Wilbarger brushes or therapeutic brushes, are designed to provide deep pressure input to the skin through brushing movements. They are often used as part of the Wilbarger Deep Pressure and Proprioceptive Technique (DPPT) to help individuals regulate sensory input.

Sensory Swings: These swings provide vestibular input and can help individuals regulate their sensory experiences. Sensory swings come in various designs, including hammock swings, platform swings, and cocoon swings.

Sensory Mats and Cushions: These mats and cushions feature different textures, materials, and sensory elements to provide tactile input and promote sensory exploration. They can be used for sitting, standing, or lying down activities.

Visual Sensory Tools: Visual sensory tools, such as bubble tubes, fiber optic lights, and lava lamps, provide calming visual input and promote relaxation. These tools are often used in sensory rooms or calming spaces.

Auditory Sensory Tools: Auditory sensory tools, such as noise-canceling headphones, white noise machines, and calming music playlists, can help individuals regulate auditory input and reduce sensitivity to noise.

Guided Imagery and Visualization Resources

Guided imagery and visualization resources can be powerful tools for promoting relaxation, reducing anxiety, and enhancing overall well-being. You can create or recommend a variety of products incorporating guided imagery and visualization techniques.

Here are some examples:

Guided Imagery Recordings: Practitioners can create audio recordings that guide clients through imaginary scenes or experiences aimed at promoting relaxation and stress reduction. These recordings typically include soothing narration, calming background music, and prompts to engage the senses. For example, a practitioner might create a guided imagery recording that takes the listener on a peaceful journey through a serene natural setting like a beach or forest.

Meditation Apps: There are many meditation apps available that offer guided imagery and visualization exercises as part of their content. Practitioners can recommend specific apps to clients or even collaborate with app developers to create customized content tailored to their therapeutic approach. These apps often include a variety of guided meditations for different purposes, such as relaxation, mindfulness, or self-compassion.

Guided Visualization Scripts: Practitioners can provide clients with written scripts for guided visualization exercises that they can practice on their own. These scripts can be tailored to address specific therapeutic goals or concerns, such as managing anxiety, improving self-esteem, or coping with chronic pain. Clients can read the scripts aloud or record themselves reading the scripts to create personalized audio recordings.

Visualization Workbooks: Practitioners can create workbooks or journals that guide clients through a series of visualization exercises designed to promote self-reflection, goal-setting, and personal growth. These workbooks often include written prompts, reflection questions, and space for clients to record their thoughts and experiences. Visualization workbooks can be used as a standalone resource or as a supplement to therapy sessions.

Virtual Reality (VR) Experiences: Virtual reality technology allows practitioners to create immersive guided imagery experiences that clients can engage with using VR headsets. These experiences can simulate peaceful natural environments, calming activities like yoga or tai chi, or interactive scenarios designed to promote relaxation and stress reduction. VR technology can provide a highly immersive and engaging way for clients to practice visualization techniques in a controlled and therapeutic environment.

Visualization Cards or Posters: Practitioners can create visual aids such as cards or posters featuring images or symbols that represent different aspects of clients' goals or aspirations. Clients can use these cards as visual prompts during guided visualization exercises to help them focus their intentions and visualize their desired outcomes. Visualization cards or posters can be especially helpful for clients who are more visually oriented or who benefit from tangible reminders of their therapeutic goals.

These guided imagery and visualization resources provide clients with practical tools and techniques for managing stress, enhancing relaxation, and fostering personal growth.

By incorporating these various tools and resources into your intensive therapy sessions and recommending them for home practice, you can empower your clients to cultivate greater self-awareness, resilience, and well-being for the long-haul, far beyond their few days with you.

There are even more ways you can enhance your standard intensive sessions beyond these products. Let's take a look at some add-on services that might benefit your clients.

Intensive Add-Ons and Supplemental Services

Additional Intensive Days of Half-Days: Perhaps there's more that you could cover with clients if they added another day or half-day to their intensive. These needs might surface from the application or during their screening call and serve as an "upsell" opportunity to address more issues at once.

Weekend Retreats: For clients who have been through your regular intensive, you might offer a multi-day program held over a weekend, providing an immersive and transformative experience away from daily distractions. This type of a retreat serves to reinforce the skills clients have learned in their individual intensives within a group format.

Follow-Up Personalized Treatment Plans: Your aftercare program is a critical tool for continuation of care beyond the intensives, but it is also a revenue generating tool. These additional sessions are scheduled after the intensive therapy experience to provide ongoing support, reinforcement, and monitoring of progress.

Holistic Wellness Activities: Integrating complementary approaches such as mindfulness practices, relaxation techniques, expressive arts therapy, or experiential exercises to promote holistic well-being is another way you can enhance and supplement your intensive.

Nutritional Counseling: We all know how important basic nutrition and diet are to our mental health, and yet it is an area that many of our clients lack foundation. Guidance on nutrition, diet, and lifestyle factors in an add-on session can enhance the effectiveness of their therapy interventions.

Accommodation and Hospitality Services: You might consider offering comfortable lodging, meals, and amenities for clients participating in multi-day intensive therapy programs, creating a supportive and nurturing environment conducive to healing. We've dedicated all of the next chapter to exploring this possibility.

Group-Based Intensives: Group intensives are a great way to increase revenue! If you have six participants, you are able to include your intensive fee along with your regular rate for each person.

Group Sessions: Your clients could really benefit from being part of a recovery community of people who understand their experiences and can support them along their journey. You might offer live or virtual group based sessions for clients to join for six weeks at a time, or longer, to focus on one particular aspect of their mental health journey.

Offering intensive therapy products and add-on services isn't just about increasing your revenue—it's about expanding the ways you can serve your clients with depth, flexibility, and creativity. From curated workbooks and post-intensive resources to aftercare check-ins and adjunct coaching, these offerings enhance the therapeutic experience while building multiple streams of income for your practice. When done thoughtfully, they not only support your clients' long-term healing but also allow your practice to thrive sustainably.

In the next chapter, we'll explore how providing a welcoming, private space for your clients to stay during their intensive can elevate their experience and open up even more possibilities for your business.

CHAPTER 28

Offering Onsite Accommodations

I never expected onsite accommodations to be such a rewarding part of my intensive therapy practice, but they are. What began as a simple solution for out-of-town clients quickly turned into something far more meaningful. I've seen firsthand how providing a quiet, welcoming space allows clients to settle in more fully, show up more authentically, and leave with a deeper sense of restoration. It's not just convenient—it's transformational.

Imagine two clients, both arriving for a 3-day intensive to confront deep-rooted patterns and begin a path toward healing.

Client A checks into a nearby hotel the night before. The front desk is busy and the lobby is noisy. They try to relax in a sterile room that smells faintly of cleaning products and yesterday's coffee. The morning of the intensive, they grab a rushed breakfast in a crowded dining area, navigate unfamiliar traffic, and arrive just in time. As we've seen from other arrival scenarios in earlier chapters, they're already a little on edge, and the chaos from the morning certainly didn't help.

Client B, on the other hand, settles into a quiet, private space onsite. The room is warm and welcoming, thoughtfully prepared with comfort and care. There's a journal on the nightstand, a stocked kitchenette, maybe even a handwritten note of encouragement. The client wakes up without the stress of a commute, takes a slow morning walk, and arrives at the intensive grounded and ready.

No matter what, both clients will do important work during the intensive, but only one has been given the gift of starting from a place of peace. That's the difference onsite accommodations can make. Let's explore how offering a place to stay can enhance your client's experience and open a new stream of income for your practice.

Onsite accommodations can provide you with more revenue, a niche offering, an immersive therapy experience, business write-offs, and convenience for your client. But don't overlook the additional professional liability, property management, local regulations, and importance of quality service that goes along with hosting your clients onsite.

For the right person or organization, onsite accommodations can be a great enhancement to your intensive practice.

Benefits and Considerations

If you're interested in offering onsite accommodations for your clients, here are some benefits and considerations to keep in mind:

Benefits for the Clinician

- **Higher Fees:** Obviously, if you are keeping your clients onsite for their intensive, you are also keeping their accommodation fees onsite as well, which means more revenue for your business!
- **Package Deals:** Onsite accommodations simplifies the process for clients, similar to an all-inclusive resort, which might attract more clients that are willing to invest in comprehensive care.
- **Niche Offering:** Providing accommodations further sets you apart from competitors who may not offer such services.
- **Brand Enhancement:** Accommodations enhance your brand as a provider of holistic and immersive therapy experiences.
- **Business Expenses:** Costs for accommodations can be considered business expenses and may be tax-deductible.

Considerations for the Clinician

- **Professional Liability:** Make sure that your professional and property liability insurance covers the extended services and accommodations.
- **Revenue Reporting:** In addition to using your property as a tax write-off, you will also need to properly report revenue generated from the accommodations to comply with tax regulations.

- **Property Management:** Managing accommodations requires additional responsibilities, including maintenance, bookings, and hospitality services. If this isn't your skill set but you still want to offer the option to your clients, you may need to hire additional staff or outsource property management to provide necessary services during the retreat.
- **Local Regulations:** Check to make sure you are in compliance with local zoning laws and health and safety regulations related to providing accommodations, and verify that offering accommodations does not conflict with your professional licensing regulations.
- **Quality of Service:** You'll want to make sure that your accommodations don't detract from but enhance the client's therapeutic experience.
- **Emergency Protocols:** Have protocols in place for handling emergencies, both medical and psychological, that may occur during their stay.
- **Privacy Concerns:** Ensure client privacy and confidentiality are maintained in the accommodation setting.

Planning Guide for Offering Onsite Accommodations

Planning your onsite accommodations isn't just about offering a place to sleep, it's about crafting an environment that supports healing, comfort, and safety from the moment your client arrives to the moment they leave. Whether you're repurposing a home, outfitting a cabin, or designing a retreat space from the ground up, every detail matters. From the layout of the property and the quality of the linens to health and safety protocols, staffing, and legal considerations, each element contributes to a seamless, restorative experience that enhances your intensive offerings.

If you're interested in offering onsite accommodations for your client, you'll want to have a plan for every critical area—from property setup to client comfort, staffing, and compliance—so you can feel confident that your accommodations are not only welcoming but well-run, professional, and therapeutically supportive. Thoughtful preparation now will pay dividends in client satisfaction, therapeutic impact, and sustainable revenue down the line.[41]

---

41 *The Onsite Accommodations Guide is included in The Intensive Method online course and is available for download from theintensivemethod.com.*

As you continue to innovate and expand your intensive practice, you might want to explore additional ways to generate revenue. In the next two chapters, we'll go over a few more options to consider beyond providing a supportive and welcoming environment for intensive work.

CHAPTER 29

Scaling Your Practice

This chapter is all about looking ahead, beyond the startup phase of your intensive therapy practice to the bright future of how you might want to scale your business. The strategies we're going to go over here will help you think about how you could diversify your practice, innovate within your practice, or grow strategically in the future.

Instead of viewing this chapter as tactical next-steps to launching your intensive, be in a dreaming / visioning frame of mind. What could the future hold for your practice?

There are three different ways to look at growth opportunities for your practice:

- Diversification
- Innovation
- Strategic Growth Initiatives

Diversification—Service Offerings Expansion

At this point you probably have at the very least an initial title and description of an intensive package in mind, potentially one for each of your target audiences. You might consider this your core offering, or your foundational intensive package, for each of your target markets.

However, there are likely many other services you could offer to these target audiences that would enrich their experience while increasing your revenue potential long term.

You might consider offering specialized programs that target specific conditions, like trauma, anxiety, PTSD, or chronic pain; group therapy sessions, which can be both cost-effective and beneficial for certain types of therapy; or workshops and seminars on mental health topics to attract new clients and retain current ones.

Another way to build upon your current intensive practice down the road is to drill down even further into different population focus areas. Here are a few examples:

- **Corporate Wellness Programs:** You might offer a version of your intensives to businesses who would like to offer mental health services as part of their employee wellness programs.
- **Veterans and First Responders:** You could create a specialized program for veterans and first responders to address their unique mental health needs.
- **Other Niche Professionals:** How might you be specially equipped to support the mental health needs of celebrities, clergy, high-profile executives, or other niche roles or industries that could benefit from your services?

We've talked about ways you can supplement your intensives with additional services in past chapters, but now is a good time to consider those services again. What services do you think would benefit your clients and be a natural add-on to your existing services? You might think about life coaching, holistic therapies, nutritional counseling, or other add-on services offered by yourself or coordinated with other healthcare providers.

Innovation—Technology Integration

Another way to grow your practice is to integrate technology. New technologies can give you a competitive edge over other practitioners and bring a new level of efficiency and efficacy to your practice.

We covered a lot of possibilities for incorporating technology into your practice from the start, but chances are some of those initiatives are more "down the road" opportunities than what you plan to do right from the beginning. Here are a few examples you might consider in the future:

- **Mobile Apps:** Develop a mobile app for booking appointments, conducting teletherapy, and providing therapeutic resources.

- **AI and Machine Learning:** Use AI to enhance diagnostic capabilities and create personalized therapy plans.
- **Virtual Reality Therapy:** Implement VR for exposure therapy and other innovative treatment methods.

We'll explore more of these technologically innovative approaches to your practice in the next chapter.

Another way to expand your practice is to invite more quantitative analysis into your counseling.

- **Outcome Tracking:** Implement software to track patient progress and outcomes, providing data to refine and improve therapy techniques.
- **Research Partnerships:** Collaborate with research institutions to stay at the forefront of therapy innovations and integrate new findings into practice.

Strategic Growth Initiatives

When you're ready to grow, there are three strategic growth initiatives you can consider:

- Geographic Expansion
- Marketing and Outreach
- Operational Efficiency

If you want to grow your business, you can always expand geographically. Intensives aren't bound by geography, but there are still geographic barriers that can limit your reach.

You could open new clinics in underserved areas to tap into new markets. You might consider franchising your practice to scale more rapidly, or you could partner with existing practices to offer your services under a co-branding arrangement. You can invite those partners to become trained in The Intensive Method so that you're able to speak the same language and take a similar approach.

It's wonderful to be able to start your business on the basis of reputation and referrals, but if you really want to put some fire behind your efforts, you will want to invest in your marketing and outreach.

We went over many of these strategies and opportunities in Part 2, but just to recap from a growth perspective, these are three main areas that can help your business expand over time:

- **Digital Marketing:** Invest in SEO, social media marketing, and online advertising to increase your practice's visibility.[42]
- **Community Engagement:** Host community events and participate in local health fairs to raise awareness of your services.
- **Referral Programs:** Develop a robust referral network with other healthcare providers, including primary care physicians and specialists.

There are other ways to grow besides getting bigger—you can also simply get better at what you currently do. As time goes by, you can make adjustments to your process that will help your business operate more efficiently, thus improving your overall practice.

Here are three ways you can improve operational efficiency:

- **Streamlined Processes:** Automate administrative tasks such as billing, scheduling, and patient records to reduce overhead.
- **Staff Training and Development:** Invest in continuous training for your staff to ensure high-quality care and improve client retention.
- **Quality Assurance Programs:** Implement quality assurance programs to maintain high standards of care.

We've dedicated all of Part 8 to continuing education, leadership formation, and professional development for the intensive practitioner.

Your strategy to grow your business will involve many of these different tactics. By combining these strategies—diversification of services, embracing innovation, and strategic growth initiatives—you can effectively scale and expand your intensive therapy practice. This multifaceted approach will help you meet the evolving needs of clients while positioning your practice for sustainable growth.

All of this talk about growing and scaling your practice might feel overwhelming at this stage of your business development, and that's perfectly normal! You might want to revisit the material in this section and the next once you've gotten at least 3-6 intensives or 3-6 months under your belt. For now, keep in mind that these are all future possibilities for down the road.

---

42 *Resources to support digital marketing and advertising your intensive are included in The Intensive Method online course and available for download at theintensivemethod.com.*

To wrap up this section, let's shift our attention to some of the ways you can enhance your practice through technological innovation.

CHAPTER 30

Innovations for Revenue Growth

Just like the different products available to optimize your practice that we covered in Chapter 27, there are also a lot of cutting-edge technologies out there that can enhance your practice… but that doesn't mean they suit every clinician. This chapter will explore some of the latest advancements in intensive therapy for those who are looking for more ways to expand revenue growth and experiment with alternative options. This isn't for everyone, though, so if VR headsets, biofeedback, and teletherapy aren't your thing, go ahead and skip this chapter.

Innovations in Intensive Therapy for Revenue Growth

The innovations we're going to cover in this chapter are all ways you can increase your revenue potential and enhance your client's experience at the same time. These are not "need-to-have" innovations, but they might be "nice-to-have" features that can set your practice apart from traditional therapy and other specialists in your area.

Let's take a look at some of the creative ways you can integrate technology into your practice and increase revenue simultaneously.

Teletherapy Platforms

While part of the power of an intensive has to do with the particular environment and time away from the client's home setting to work on their challenges in-person, practitioners can take advantage of teletherapy platforms to bring in family members during an intensive.

Including a family member virtually can provide valuable insights into family dynamics and relationships. A Zoom call or teletherapy session can allow you to observe interactions between family members in real-time, so that you can facilitate a deeper understanding of familial issues and dynamics.

It also allows you to invite a family member in for collaborative problem solving and goal setting without the expense or expectation of being present for the full 3-day intensive. Family members can contribute their perspectives and insights, leading to more comprehensive and effective treatment plans as well as greater buy-in for support once the client returns home.

Sometimes a client can benefit from having a supportive presence in the room, even if they are virtual. Having a familiar face present can help the client feel more comfortable and supported during the therapeutic process.

You could also consider their at-home clinician calling into a session or a sponsor if they're in recovery, or maybe a close friend, if there is a relational situation that needs to be processed.

Virtual Reality Therapy

While I don't have much virtual reality experience, personally or professionally, our research has surfaced some interesting information I would like to share with you. Virtual reality (VR) therapy offers immersive experiences for clients dealing with anxiety, phobias, PTSD, and other mental health issues. Practitioners can incorporate VR into their practice, attracting clients seeking innovative and effective treatment methods.

VR therapy is an emerging field, offering lots of dynamic and exciting possibilities for the future of therapy. Here are a few interesting ways VR therapy can be used:

Exposure Therapy: VR exposure therapy is often used to treat phobias, anxiety disorders, and PTSD by exposing individuals to virtual simulations of mild to moderately triggering stimuli in a controlled environment. For example, someone with a fear of heights can undergo VR exposure therapy by gradually exposing themselves to virtual heights until their anxiety diminishes.

Stress Reduction and Relaxation: VR environments can be designed to promote relaxation and stress reduction. Individuals can immerse themselves in calming virtual environments such as peaceful landscapes or tranquil scenes, allowing them to practice mindfulness and relaxation techniques.

Pain Management: VR therapy has been shown to help manage chronic pain by distracting individuals from their discomfort and promoting relaxation. VR experiences can transport individuals to immersive virtual worlds, diverting their attention away from physical pain and reducing the need for pain medication.

Social Skills Training: VR can be used to facilitate social skills training for individuals with autism spectrum disorder (ASD) or social anxiety disorder. Virtual simulations allow individuals to practice social interactions in a safe and controlled environment, helping them develop and improve their social skills.

Cognitive Rehabilitation: VR therapy can be used in cognitive rehabilitation programs for individuals with brain injuries or cognitive impairments. Virtual exercises and simulations are designed to improve cognitive functions such as attention, memory, problem-solving, and executive functioning.

Mindfulness and Meditation: VR applications can guide individuals through mindfulness and meditation practices by immersing them in serene virtual environments and providing audiovisual cues for relaxation and breathing exercises.

Virtual Reality Exposure for Substance Use Disorders (VR-SUD): VR-SUD therapy exposes individuals with substance use disorders to virtual environments that simulate real-world scenarios involving drug or alcohol cues. This form of exposure therapy helps individuals develop coping strategies and reduce cravings in high-risk situations.

Phantom Limb Pain Management: VR therapy has shown promise in treating phantom limb pain by providing immersive experiences that help individuals alleviate sensations related to missing limbs. Virtual simulations can trick the brain into perceiving movement and sensations in the phantom limb, reducing pain and discomfort.

You can read more about the potential benefits of using virtual reality in therapy in "Virtual reality as a clinical tool in mental health research and practice," published in *Dialogues in Clinical Neuroscience*, June 22, 2020.[43]

---

43 *https://www.ncbi.nlm.nih.gov/pmc/articles/PMC7366939/*

Biofeedback Devices

Another technological advance you can use in your intensive practice is biofeedback.

Biofeedback devices measure physiological responses such as heart rate, skin conductance, and muscle tension. Practitioners can incorporate biofeedback into their practice to help clients learn self-regulation techniques and monitor progress. Clients who are especially fond of new tech, data, and gadgets may benefit from this kind of technology integration.[44]

Artificial Intelligence (AI) in Therapy

We're all just beginning to scratch the surface of the power of artificial intelligence in therapy. AI-powered tools can help practitioners analyze large amounts of data to provide insights into clients' behavior patterns and treatment progress. Practitioners can leverage AI for personalized treatment plans and interventions, improving outcomes, and attracting clients seeking tailored therapeutic approaches. AI can offer data analysis and insights, neuro-linguistic programming (NLP), chatbots and virtual assistants, predictive analytics, personalized treatment plans, emotion recognition and sentiment analysis, and more.

It's a brave new world, my friends! Remember to check with your boards and regulation organizations to protect yourself and your clients as you explore new technologies.

Mindfulness and Meditation Programs

Integrating mindfulness and meditation programs into intensive therapy sessions can help clients manage stress, improve focus, and enhance overall well-being. These add-ons could be conducted by you, another member of your staff, or offered in app form. Therapists can offer specialized programs or workshops to attract clients interested in holistic approaches to mental health.

Collaborative Care Models

Partnering with other healthcare providers, such as primary care physicians or psychiatrists, in collaborative care models can expand your referral networks

---

44 *For more ways biofeedback devices have been used to treat various conditions, read this Medical News Today article: https://www.medicalnewstoday.com/articles/265802*

and revenue streams. By offering integrated services, practitioners can attract clients seeking comprehensive mental health support.

It seems like something shiny and new is being developed and released every week! Like I said at the beginning of this chapter, these are all "nice-to-have," not "must-have," options. If you aren't that interested in new tech, don't feel like you have to rely on these additional innovations in order to enhance your business. If you DO love technology, go for it! Just don't go too crazy all at once—try out something new here and there so as not to overwhelm yourself, your clients, or your staff. Give anything new some time to be tested and tweaked before you decide whether to keep it or throw it out.

In the last section, we will turn our attention to your own personal and professional development. I want you to feel equipped and confident to deliver effective intensives, no matter what area of specialization you have, so that you can thrive in your practice.

PART 8

The Long Game

CHAPTER 31

Professional Growth and Supervision

Beyond your own self-care plan, which is an important part of any practitioner's routine, is the development of a reflective practice for your business. Developing a reflective practice involves regularly examining your therapeutic approach, your interactions with clients, and your emotional responses to therapy sessions.

This self-assessment process allows you to identify areas of strength and opportunities for improvement.

When offering intensive therapy, it's crucial to maintain a high level of self-awareness and professional integrity. Regularly setting aside time for reflection helps you stay aligned with best practices, ensures ethical standards, and enhances your ability to deliver effective and empathetic care.

Techniques for Engaging in Reflective Practice

Here are several different ways you can regularly reflect on how you and your practice are doing:

Journaling: Maintain a regular journal where you document your thoughts, feelings, and reactions after each therapy session. Note what went well, what could be improved, and any significant insights gained.

Structured Reflection: Use specific frameworks like Gibbs' Reflective Cycle or Schön's Reflective Practice model to systematically analyze your experiences.[45] This structured approach can help you delve deeper into your practice. There is no right or perfect structure for reflection; find the model that works best for you.

Case Reviews: Periodically review and analyze case notes and session recordings. Reflect on your interventions, the client's progress, and any challenges faced.

Mindfulness and Meditation: Engage in mindfulness practices to enhance your self-awareness and emotional regulation. This can help you remain present and reflective in your professional and personal life.

Peer Reflection Groups: Form or join a group of peers where you can discuss and reflect on your practice. Sharing experiences with colleagues can provide new perspectives and insights.

Self-Assessment Tools

Beyond reflective practices, you can also use a variety of self-assessment tools to help you gain perspective and deepen your self-awareness.

Self-Evaluation Tools: Use self-assessment questionnaires and tools specific to your therapy practice to evaluate your competencies, areas for growth, and professional development needs.

Goal Setting: Set specific, measurable goals for your professional development. Regularly review and adjust these goals based on your self-assessment outcomes.

Client Feedback: Solicit regular feedback from your clients about their experiences and progress in therapy. Use this feedback to reflect on your effectiveness and identify areas for improvement.

Video/Audio Review: Record your therapy sessions (with client consent) and review them to self-assess your communication skills, therapeutic techniques, and client interactions.

Continuing Education: Engage in ongoing education and training to stay updated with the latest research and techniques in intensive therapy. Reflect on how these new learnings can be integrated into your practice.

---

45 *Guidelines for these models are included in The Intensive Method online course and are available for download at theintensivemethod.com.*

Consultation

We all can use outside input to help us grow. Being receptive to feedback can be challenging, especially if you've been operating in your own practice for a long time. However, feedback from others can lead to continuous growth and improvement in your professional practice. Here are some tips to integrate consultation into your reflective practice:

Regular Supervision or Consultation Sessions: Schedule consistent and frequent sessions with a qualified supervisor or consultant. Use these sessions to discuss challenging cases, receive feedback, and explore your own responses and feelings.

Supervision or Consultation Contracts: Establish clear contracts that outline the goals, expectations, and boundaries of the relationship. This can help ensure productive and focused sessions.

Case Presentations: Prepare detailed case presentations for your sessions. This can help you articulate your thought process and receive targeted feedback.

Reflective Supervision: Engage in reflective supervision where the focus is not only on case management but also on understanding your own emotional and cognitive processes. This can help deepen your self-awareness and professional growth.

Action Plans: Develop action plans based on the feedback and guidance received during your meetings. Implement these plans in your practice and review them in subsequent sessions to track your progress.

Actively seeking supervision and consultation from seasoned professionals provides valuable external perspectives on difficult cases and professional dilemmas. Engaging with mentors and industry experts helps you navigate both clinical and business aspects of intensive therapy. These relationships offer a supportive space to discuss therapeutic techniques, client dynamics, and personal reactions, helping to prevent burnout and maintain a high quality of care.

Supervision or consultation is included as part of certification and membership in The Intensive Method. More information about this program can be found at theintensivemethod.com.

Creating a Reflective Practice Routine

The frequency with which a practitioner should engage in reflective practices can vary depending on your experience level, the intensity of your caseload, and your personal and professional development needs. Here are some general guidelines that can help you determine the best structure for your reflective practice routine:

Daily Reflection: Brief daily reflections can be highly beneficial. This can be done through journaling or spending a few minutes at the end of each day to think about the sessions held, personal reactions, and any immediate learning points.

Weekly Reflection: A more in-depth reflective session once a week allows for a comprehensive review of the week's work. This can involve revisiting case notes, assessing progress towards professional goals, and planning for future sessions.

Immediate Reflection: Engage in a quick reflection after each therapy session. This can help capture immediate thoughts and feelings, assess what worked well, and identify any aspects that could be improved for future sessions.

Monthly or Bi-Monthly Consultation Supervision Sessions: Therapists might meet with their supervisors monthly or bi-monthly, but those dealing with more complex cases or intensive therapy formats might benefit from more frequent consultation.

Collaboration and Consultation for Coaches: Coaches might meet regularly with other practitioners in their niche for collaboration and consultation to help determine when a referral might be appropriate.

Quarterly Reviews: Conduct a more extensive review every three months to evaluate your overall progress, revisit professional goals, and make necessary adjustments to your practice. This periodical reflection can help in identifying long-term trends and patterns in your practice.

Annual Self-Assessment and Planning: At least once a year, engage in a thorough self-assessment and professional development planning session. This could include reflecting on the past year's achievements, setting new goals, and planning further training or continuing education.

During Significant Changes or Challenges Critical Reflection: Increase the frequency of reflective practices during times of significant change or when facing particular challenges. This could be when dealing with a particularly difficult case, during major transitions in your practice, or after receiving significant feedback from supervision.

Examples of Routine Integration

Here's a boiled down version of what your reflective routine could look like:

Daily Journaling: Spend 10-15 minutes at the end of each day writing about your sessions.

Weekly Group Reflection: Join or form a peer supervision group that meets weekly to discuss and reflect on cases.

Monthly Supervision Sessions: Schedule a regular monthly meeting with a supervisor to discuss ongoing cases and professional development.

Quarterly Workshops: Attend or organize quarterly workshops or training sessions that encourage reflective practice.

No matter what routine you establish, reflection should be an integral part of your routine rather than an occasional activity. Integrate reflective practices into your daily schedule in a way that they become habitual.

Integrating Feedback and Insights into Your Practice

The process of supervision and mentorship is not complete without the application of received feedback and insights. After discussions with supervisors and mentors, it's essential to integrate their advice and observations into your therapeutic practice along with any insights you've gathered from your own personal self-reflection and assessment.

This may involve adopting new strategies, modifying existing techniques, or addressing specific areas for growth. Continuously refining your skills based on this feedback leads to better client outcomes and enhances your professional development. Regularly updating your practice based on supervision insights ensures that you remain responsive to client needs and adaptive to the evolving landscape of intensive therapy.

Learning to accept constructive feedback can be challenging. It takes time out of your busy schedule and requires an openness to what might feel like criticism. As we often suggest with our clients, we should intentionally reframe this as an opportunity for growth or change, not a criticism. In fact we are all learning as we go, so be sure to check in with yourself to be sure, if you have internal resistance, to find ways now to overcome those struggles.

The demand for quality intensive therapy is high—people need the help that we can give them! If you're doing your job well and word starts to get out, you're going to need to find ways to manage business growth without compromising your client's experience.

In our next chapter, we'll talk about strategies and tactics to manage the next level of business growth in your intensive therapy practice. Once again, you will want to take a visionary dreamer posture in this chapter. Now is the time to imagine the possibilities, not get overwhelmed by what ifs. As already mentioned, and worth repeating, this material will come in handy several months or even years into your practice's growth, so don't hesitate to circle back to this material later on, when you're ready to take your business to the next level.

CHAPTER 32

Leadership and Team Building

If anyone at all helps you run your practice, this chapter will offer you some business management tips for leading and managing people. Even if you don't hire full- or part-time staff, at some point you may choose to work with a contractual support team to help you accomplish your goals, like we covered in earlier chapters. If you want your practice to succeed, you'll need to be able to manage those individuals well.

In this chapter, we're going to look at five different areas of managerial leadership:

- Leadership and communication skills
- Building relationships and team dynamics
- Employee development and empowerment
- Performance management and feedback
- Decision-making and problem solving

Leadership and Communication Skills

If you're used to flying solo, the whole team of people that needs to know what you're thinking lives inside your head. You know your vision and your goals. You are aware of the "why" behind different tasks and responsibilities.

But once you invite even one more person into your operation, the dynamics change. You are the leader. How will you lead?

As people in the mental health field, we already know how important communication is, but that doesn't mean we're always great at practicing what we preach. As a manager, you'll want to develop strong communication skills to share your expectations, provide people feedback, and foster a positive work environment. This includes active listening, clear articulation of goals and objectives, and empathy in understanding your team's needs and concerns.

We also know good communication isn't just what you say, it's how you say it... and not to mention making sure what needs to be communicated is in fact, just that, communicated. Be sure to implement effective communication by specifically defining *when* you will communicate with your team, *what* you will be communicating with your team, and *how* you will communicate the information.

For example, you may decide to have weekly meetings. Will those be live meetings, phone meetings, or virtual meetings? Will you set the agenda yourself, ask for input, or just wing the meetings? And lastly, how will important information be exchanged? Will you take notes, use email, employ AI summary tools, or have an online platform, like Slack, to organize and disseminate important information? You may utilize all of these measures, but take a moment to pause and consider your preferred methods as well as your team members' and begin to develop a communication strategy.

Inspiring Vision: Simon Sinek, author and inspirational speaker on business leadership, made purpose-driven leadership famous in his book, *Start with Why*. Your "why" is the foundation of your practice. Sinek writes, "When we know WHY we do what we do, everything falls into place. When we don't, we have to push things into place."

What is the reason you believe in this work? Why should your team care? Using the tips about developing your brand identity in Chapter 7 as a guide, articulate a compelling vision for the practice and inspire your team to align with your organizational mission and values. Communicate the bigger picture to cultivate a sense of purpose and ownership in your team's work.

If you take your work seriously, your team is more likely to take their work seriously. If you bring joy and optimism to your practice, your team is more likely to be joyful and optimistic. Demonstrate leadership qualities through your actions and behaviors.

Building Relationships and Team Dynamics

If you have more than one person on your team helping you out, well, now you have a crowd. More people means more personalities and more potential—for conflict, sure, but also for exponentially greater creativity and growth. It can be challenging to manage the relationships on a team, especially if many of your team members serve your organization remotely, but it is definitely possible.

I've seen it work firsthand—in fact, The Intensive Method is the product of a dynamic team of women working together across several different states!

When you're leading a group of people, these tenets will help you be successful:

Create a Supportive Culture: Foster a culture of trust, respect, and collaboration within the team. Encourage open communication, mutual support, and a sense of camaraderie among staff members.

Team-Building Activities: If your team is local and able to meet in-person, organize team-building activities and events to strengthen relationships and promote teamwork. This can include group outings, team-building exercises, or regular team meetings to foster connections and camaraderie. If your support team is mostly or exclusively virtual, schedule regular video-based calls for the whole team as well as one-on-one check-ins to maintain rapport and listen to what your colleagues have to say. This is especially important when email or text threads lack the nuance of tone of voice and body language to convey what we mean effectively.

Conflict Resolution: It's going to happen—we're humans! We are wired differently. We have conflicting opinions and personalities. It's important to recognize this and develop strategies for managing conflicts and resolving interpersonal issues within the team. Facilitate constructive dialogue, address conflicts promptly and fairly, and promote a culture of understanding and reconciliation.

You might consider using a self-assessment personality profile to give vocabulary to the ways in which different members of your team are wired. Myers-Briggs, Clifton Strengths, SDI (Strengths Deployment Inventory), and the Enneagram are four such tools that can illuminate the differences between team members and how they view the world. Use the tool that seems the most supportive of your team's issues and dynamics.[46]

Employee Development and Empowerment

As someone who is used to doing it all, it can be particularly challenging to trust new people with the tasks you used to do and the material you know inside and out. But in order for your team to be effective—and for you to not burnout—you have to be able to empower your team with both the responsibility and the appropriate authority to do their jobs. Here are some ways you can help facilitate that process:

Training and Development: Invest in training and development programs to enhance your team's skills and competencies. This is more appropriate for someone who is on your paid staff than a consultant or contract worker, whom you've hired explicitly for their existing expertise. However, when you first invite a new contractor into your organization, be sure to invest time and energy into their onboarding so they grasp as well as they can just what it is you do and how your business is wired. This will help them be successful and you trust their work.

Delegating Responsibilities: Delegate tasks and responsibilities effectively to empower staff and foster a sense of ownership and accountability. Provide clear guidance and resources, while also allowing autonomy and decision-making authority where appropriate.

Recognition and Reward: Everyone likes an atta-boy or atta-girl! Acknowledge and celebrate your team members' achievements and contributions. Implement recognition programs, rewards, and incentives to motivate and inspire their performance. A little bit here can go a long way.

Performance Management and Feedback

In addition to recognition for a job well done, it's also important to manage your team's performance by providing feedback and setting expectations as you go along. This is true whether they are regular staff members or contractual employees.

---

46 *More information about these four self-assessments is included in The Intensive Method online course and is available for download at theintensivemethod.com.*

Set Clear Expectations: Establish clear performance expectations and standards for your team members. If you are hiring contractual workers, make sure that you set some kind of upfront contract that clearly articulates what they are responsible for doing. Define measurable goals and objectives, and provide regular feedback on performance to ensure alignment with your practice's objectives. Ongoing feedback and coaching supports your team's development and improvement. Offer constructive feedback, identify areas for growth, and provide resources and support to help them succeed.

Performance Reviews: For team members who are regular employees, conduct regular performance evaluations to assess their progress and performance. Use performance reviews as an opportunity to recognize achievements, address areas for improvement, and set goals for future development.

With contractual employees, you might instead schedule a check-in for various intervals, at the start of a project, monthly throughout the duration of the project, and prior to renewing any agreements so that you can set or reset expectations and monitor progress together.

Ultimately, the goal of these endeavors is to encourage your team members, to keep the crew pointed in the same direction, and to ensure that your team is in alignment with your mission and vision. Your actual interactions dealing with the day-to-day tasks and obstacles are all serving this broader goal, even when the team isn't necessarily aware of it. But you are, and it's your job to keep that vision within your team's sight.

Decision-Making and Problem-Solving

Again, when it's just you managing your business without any other colleagues, problems that arise are solved by *you*. Decisions that need to be made are made by *you*. This shifts as soon as you have additional help, even if ever so slightly. Sure, you could keep managing your business as if you're the only one whose opinion counts—and decisions ultimately come back to you—but a strong leader involves their team in operational decisions instead of running their business like a dictatorship.

Involving team members in the decision-making process fosters a sense of ownership and commitment. More input, diverse perspectives, and collaboration means greater consensus and better solutions.

When challenges and obstacles within the practice arise, analyze them systematically. Resist the urge to make knee-jerk decisions. Often, repeat problems are symptoms of a deeper issue. Dig underneath the surface of problems to identify their root causes, and implement effective solutions to overcome barriers and drive improvement.

Remain adaptable and flexible in your approach to decision-making and problem-solving. With a team of people, it's important to be open to new ideas, feedback, and alternative solutions. If you remain nimble and able to adjust course as needed to address changing circumstances and priorities, your team and your business will flourish.

Adding more voices into the management and operations of your business is a new challenge but one that comes with great rewards. You will learn more things about the human experience and grow as a professional along the way!

In the next chapter, we're going to look at additional ways you can expand your expertise and enhance your practice through continuing education and professional development opportunities. As you look for future ways to enrich your expertise, this chapter will help you discern which training, specializations, and certifications are worth investing in to enhance your practice.

CHAPTER 33

Continuing Education and Specialization

Kara had high hopes when she signed up for a weekend workshop. The title promised "Advanced Techniques for Deep Transformation" and boasted a faculty of seasoned clinicians. As a licensed therapist eager to expand her intensive offerings, she was excited by the possibility of learning new interventions and adding credibility to her practice.

She paid nearly $1,000 for the training, plus travel and hotel, but by the end of the first day, something felt off. The sessions were mostly lecture-based with very little hands-on application. The examples were vague and didn't align with the structure or depth she knew intensives required. The presenters, while experienced, didn't specialize in intensives, and it showed. There was no discussion of pacing over multiple days, no content on how to manage client fatigue, and no strategies for integrating clinical documentation or aftercare.

By Sunday afternoon, Kara sat in the closing circle with a certificate in her bag, but no real takeaways she could implement on Monday. She left feeling frustrated at both the lost time and money.

As you look to the future for ways to enhance your intensive practice, you'll discover that there are lots of different options out there for training and certifications. These additional credentials can help set you apart from other practitioners, further diversifying your offerings.

There are several important questions to ask yourself before you embark on new opportunities, because just like Kara's scenario illustrates, not every training is created equal.

How to Choose from New Trainings and Certifications

Educational Content vs. Protocol Guidance

First, consider whether the training is educational content or protocol guidance. Does this training or certification teach you about the topic or does it provide a specifically outlined protocol, or does it do both? If it does both, how much protocol is included? How robust and plug-and-play is it?

Understanding whether a training offers theoretical knowledge, practical application, or both will help you determine if it meets your learning needs and how you can implement it in your practice. A balance of both can be particularly beneficial, offering comprehensive education and actionable steps.

Client Awareness and Value Perception

Next, think about how the training or certification will be perceived by your clients.

Would clients know to look for this certification or training? Client awareness of the certification can impact its perceived value and attractiveness. If clients recognize and value the certification, it can enhance your credibility and marketability, potentially leading to increased client acquisition.

Does it establish a specialty that would give a return on the investment? Specializations can differentiate a practitioner in a competitive market and justify the cost of the training through higher fees, increased client base, or more effective treatments, ultimately leading to a return on investment.

Revenue Potential

Does the training provide certifications that bolster your credentials? If clients don't understand what the initials mean, will it help convert or show value at first sight?

You need to be able to balance your desire for knowledge with your practical need for income. Trainings that do not convert to revenue might still be valuable for professional growth but should be weighed against those that offer both knowledge and financial benefits.

Practical Business Tools

Practical business tools enhance the immediate applicability of new knowledge, allowing you to streamline your operations and improve client offerings without a lengthy adaptation period. This can lead to quick improvements in service quality and client satisfaction.

Does the training deliver great content and also provide plug-and-play business tools that can immediately improve processes and client offerings? Is it easy to market to clients, showing them what they will get for their money?

The ability to communicate the benefits of new certifications or trainings to clients is crucial. If clients understand the value proposition, they are more likely to engage with the services, leading to better client retention and acquisition.

Implementation Support

Certifications can be helpful in establishing reputation and referrals. However, some organizations provide certifications that teach you a lot about a topic but lack business tools like treatment plans, interventions, assessments, marketing materials, technology tools, etc.

Can you implement what you've learned effectively, or do you feel frustrated and unsure of how to proceed after spending a lot of money on training?

Comprehensive certifications that include practical tools for implementation ensure that you can effectively integrate new knowledge into your practice. Without these tools, there is a risk of frustration and underutilization of the training, leading to wasted resources and missed opportunities for practice improvement.

We've tried to make The Intensive Method the kind of training that allows you to implement a delivery method for therapy with plenty of practical resources so you can hit the ground running. Our goal has been to provide practitioners with everything they need so they truly can jump right into promoting and offering intensives with as much ease as possible.

TIM: Double-Niched Practitioner

The Intensive Method is going to give you the structure and medium to deliver something that is specialized. If you can add other areas of expertise to your intensive offerings, you will be double niched and prepared to deliver a unique therapeutic process to meet clients' needs.

Let's imagine that you've been successfully running your practice using The Intensive Method. You offer structured, immersive therapeutic sessions designed to address complex client issues over a concentrated period. While your clients benefit from the focused nature of TIM, you see an opportunity to enhance your offerings by incorporating additional specializations.

You recently attended a professional development workshop on Dialectical Behavior Therapy (DBT), a highly effective treatment for clients with emotional regulation issues, such as those with borderline personality disorder or chronic suicidality. Impressed by DBT's structured approach, which combines cognitive-behavioral techniques with mindfulness practices, you immediately see its potential to complement your intensive therapy offerings.

Inspired by the workshop, you decide to integrate DBT into your practice. You envision a 3-day intensive DBT program that leverages the strengths of both TIM and DBT to provide a powerful therapeutic experience.

You spend some time with the TIM resources to plan and outline how you'll structure and deliver your DBT program over the course of three days.

You draft a value proposition and clearly articulate the unique benefits of combining TIM with DBT. Your messaging focuses on the rapid progress clients can achieve through this structured and evidence-based approach.

Your first client for the new program is a young woman struggling with severe anxiety and emotional dysregulation. She has tried traditional weekly therapy but feels she needs more immediate and intensive support. By the end of the 3-day program, your client has made significant strides in managing her emotions and improving her relationships. She feels empowered by the skills she has learned and is grateful for the intensive support she received.

Your decision to integrate DBT with The Intensive Method has not only expanded your professional expertise but also provided your clients with a more robust therapeutic experience. The new 3-day intensive DBT program offers a unique and highly effective solution for individuals seeking immediate and comprehensive support for their emotional and behavioral challenges.

This is of course just one possible therapeutic approach out of many that could be integrated with The Intensive Method.

Trainings and Certifications That Pair Well with The Intensive Method

Chapter 11 explored various tools and modalities that might pair well with your intensive practice and enhance your specialization.[47]

In addition to these approaches, the Hope & Freedom Institute offers a training that builds upon the skills you've learned in The Intensive Method to become a Certified Hope and Freedom Practitioner (CHFP). CHFPs are specially trained in sex addiction and betrayal trauma to facilitate intensive therapy for individuals and couples who struggle with compulsive sexual behavior and its ramifications on relationships. We believe Hope & Freedom's approach to treating individuals in these situations is an effective way to stop sex addiction and heal from betrayal trauma. If this is an area of specialty you want to explore, visit the Hope & Freedom Institute website at hopeandfreedom.net to learn more.

After completing The Intensive Method initial course to become a CHFP, you'll complete additional hours of hands-on training and 1-1 mentorship onsite at Hope & Freedom's main location. Similar tools, systems, forms, and marketing materials like what we offer through The Intensive Method online course are also included, specifically designed for CHFPs.

Regardless of your specialization interests, I hope you are able to see just how adaptable The Intensive Method can be for your practice. Soon, I'm confident you'll see how effective this method is for your clients!

47 *A handout on these therapeutic tools and modalities is included in The Intensive Method online course and is available for download at theintensivemethod.com.*

CHAPTER 34

Creative Expansion and Flexibility

I strongly believe that you have what it takes to launch an innovative, effective intensive practice. The fact that you picked up this book alone indicates that you possess an entrepreneurial spirit. But as a practitioner launching a new component to your practice—or maybe a new practice altogether—there are bound to be some bumps in the road.

These four elements are critical to your success as a practitioner of intensives:

- Embracing Change
- Navigating Uncertainty
- Building Resilience
- Fostering Creativity

Now, you may be thinking, *Tina, this is what I do, every single day with my clients. In one way, shape, or form, I teach them how to embrace change, navigate uncertainty, build resilience, and foster creativity. I'm a pro at these things!*

This is probably true, but how often are you able to apply these truths and practices to your own life? Sometimes, we need some reminders. Let's take a closer look at these four elements of leadership and why they're so important in the intensive setting.

Embracing Change

As your intensive practice grows, it's important to pay attention to shifts in the needs and preferences of your clients.

In recent years, for example, more and more clients are expressing a desire for virtual therapy sessions due to convenience, accessibility, and privacy concerns. There's also been a surge in demand for the integration of holistic approaches to mental health and wellness, including mindfulness, yoga, and art therapy.

Fads will come and go, new research and therapeutic innovations will emerge, trends will ebb and flow. Embracing change is crucial in our industry for several reasons:

Client-Centered Approach: Your primary focus should always be on meeting the evolving needs of your clients. By recognizing the dynamic nature of the mental health landscape, you can adapt your practice to offer services that align with what your clients are seeking.

Competitive Advantage: In a rapidly changing industry, staying ahead of the curve can give you a competitive edge. Embracing change allows you to differentiate your practice by offering innovative therapies that address emerging client needs.

Market Relevance: To remain relevant in the market, you must stay informed about industry developments and market trends. This awareness enables you to anticipate changes and proactively adapt your practice to meet the demands of the market.

Professional Growth: Embracing change fosters professional growth and development. It encourages you and your team to continuously learn new techniques, stay updated on research findings, and explore innovative approaches to therapy.

Ethical Responsibility: As a leader in the mental health community, you have an ethical responsibility to provide the best possible care to your clients. Embracing change allows you to integrate evidence-based practices and adapt to advancements in the field, ensuring that you're offering the most effective treatments available.

As more individuals desire access to in-depth mental health options, the demand for intensive therapy is only going to increase. You're now positioned to meet the needs of clients in this innovative way and be a pioneer in this field!

Navigating Uncertainty

As a leader in your practice, you are bound to encounter uncertainties.

Regulatory changes, economic factors, technological advancements, societal trends, and public health crises are all external sources of uncertainty that could impact your practice.

Internally, changes to your team, funding uncertainty, variability in client outcomes, unexpected treatment responses, or competition and market dynamics can also impact your practice.

None of us are immune to these uncertainties. Here are some strategies to help navigate these situations:

Maintain a Growth Mindset: Encourage yourself and your team to adopt a growth mindset, which involves embracing challenges as opportunities for growth and learning. Instead of viewing uncertainty as a threat, see it as a chance to develop new skills, try different approaches, and adapt to change.

Seek Opportunities for Learning and Innovation: Actively seek out opportunities for learning and innovation within your practice. This could involve attending conferences, workshops, or seminars to stay updated on the latest research and trends in therapy. Encourage your team to share ideas and experiment with new techniques or approaches to therapy.

Stay Agile in Decision-Making: In uncertain and ambiguous situations, it's essential to remain flexible and agile in your decision-making process. Avoid getting stuck in rigid plans or strategies that may no longer be effective. Instead, be willing to adjust your course of action based on new information, feedback, or changing circumstances.

Foster Open Communication: Create a culture of open communication within your practice where team members feel comfortable sharing their ideas, concerns, and feedback. Encourage brainstorming sessions and collaborative problem-solving to generate innovative solutions to challenges.

Develop Contingency Plans: Anticipate potential challenges or obstacles that may arise in uncertain situations and develop contingency plans to address them. Having backup strategies in place can help mitigate risks and provide a sense of reassurance during times of uncertainty.

Embrace Failure as a Learning Opportunity: Encourage a culture where failure is seen as a natural part of the learning process. Instead of being discouraged by setbacks, use them as opportunities to reflect, learn, and grow. Celebrate small successes and milestones along the way to maintain morale and motivation.

By incorporating these strategies into your practice, you can effectively manage uncertainty and ambiguity, maintain a growth mindset, seek opportunities for learning and innovation, and stay agile in decision-making.

Building Resilience

Building resilience is essential for practitioners working with The Intensive Method. You will likely face high levels of stress, emotional intensity, and challenging client cases on a regular basis. By now, the following practices are probably obvious to you, but no matter how many times we've heard it, putting these habits into action is always harder.

Here are some strategies for developing resilience and coping mechanisms to overcome setbacks, challenges, and unexpected obstacles in your practice journey:

Self-Care Practices: Prioritize self-care activities such as regular exercise, healthy eating, adequate sleep, and relaxation techniques like mindfulness or meditation. Taking care of your physical and emotional well-being is crucial for maintaining resilience in the face of stress.

Seeking Support: Seek support from colleagues, supervisors, or external mentors. Having a supportive network of peers who understand the unique challenges of intensive therapy work can provide validation, perspective, and emotional support during difficult times.

Setting Boundaries: Establish clear boundaries between work and personal life to prevent burnout and maintain a healthy work-life balance. Schedule regular breaks, vacations, and time for leisure activities to recharge and replenish your energy reserves. Remember the time management and scheduling principles we went over earlier and follow them.

Practicing Mindfulness: Use mindfulness techniques to help yourself stay present, calm, and focused amidst the chaos of intensive therapy work. Mindfulness practices can help reduce stress, improve emotional regulation, and enhance overall well-being.

Building Resilient Thinking Patterns: Develop resilient thinking patterns by challenging negative beliefs, reframing setbacks as learning opportunities, and cultivating a growth mindset. Try to recognize your own strengths, accomplishments, and successes, even in the face of adversity.

Cultivating Meaning and Purpose: When you've had a difficult client experience or feel particularly challenged by the work you're doing, return to your values, passions, and motivations for what you're doing in order to cultivate a sense of meaning and purpose in your work. Remember why you're doing what you're doing and recall the positive impact you've had on your clients' lives. You are making a meaningful contribution in the world of mental health!

Building resilience not only supports your own well-being but also enhances your ability to provide effective and compassionate care to your clients.

Fostering Creativity

Continuing to foster the sense of creativity that you've brought to your practice already will bring lasting joy and innovation to your practice and better outcomes for your clients. Here are some strategies to maintain that culture of creativity and experimentation:

Encourage Open Communication: If you do have others on your team, create an environment where team members feel comfortable sharing their ideas, opinions, and feedback openly. Encourage brainstorming sessions, team meetings, and forums for discussing new ideas and approaches to therapy.

Celebrate Diversity of Perspectives: Recognize and value the diversity of perspectives, backgrounds, and experiences within your team. Encourage practitioners to draw on their unique insights and expertise to inform their therapeutic approaches and problem-solving strategies. If you are a solo-practitioner, you can seek out diverse perspectives in your research, media consumption, and reading. Follow diverse voices on social media. Watch diverse perspectives in videos. Register for webinars and workshops from different points of view than your own. Allow these differing perspectives to shape and challenge your own way of thinking and practicing. Your openness will be rewarded!

Provide Resources and Support: Don't limit those perspectives to yourself. Offer resources, training opportunities, and professional development support to empower your team to explore new techniques, modalities, and interventions. Provide access to research literature, workshops, conferences, and peer consultation groups to inspire creativity and innovation.

Embrace Risk-Taking and Experimentation: Keep taking calculated risks and experimenting with new ideas, techniques, and interventions in your clinical practice. Again, failure is a natural part of the learning process and an opportunity for growth and innovation.

Create Space for Reflection and Creativity: Provide dedicated time and space to reflect on your work, explore creative ideas, and engage in self-directed learning. Use journaling, artistic expression, and other creative outlets as tools for self-discovery and inspiration, and prompt your team to do the same.

Lead by Example: Your team will pick up on what really matters to you, so demonstrate a commitment to creativity and innovation as a leader by modeling curiosity, openness to new ideas, and willingness to experiment. Share your own experiences of creative problem-solving and encourage others to follow suit.

Recognize and Reward Creativity: Acknowledge and celebrate instances of creativity, innovation, and successful experimentation within the practice.

Cultivating creativity not only enriches the therapeutic experience for clients but will also keep you energized and inspired.

Uncertainty and the need for change is bound to come as you embark on this next adventure. Embrace it! You already have the skills you need to overcome unexpected obstacles in your practice.

CHAPTER 35

Conclusion: Building a Life and Business You Love

You made it. You've worked your way through this guide on how to offer 3-day intensives with clarity, excellence, and confidence. You've explored the framework, structure, tools, and mindset that make this work both clinically effective and deeply transformative. From intake to aftercare, from marketing to time management, you've equipped yourself with everything you need to build something remarkable.

So before we go any further—pause and celebrate that.

You've invested in yourself, your clients, and your future. Now, as we close, I want to take a moment to end on a personal note. I'd like to tell you a little more about where The Intensive Method came from, and why this isn't just a model to me—it's a mission.

Hope & Freedom was my entry point. I was personally mentored into intensive work by Dr. Milton Magness, the founder of Hope & Freedom Counseling Services, and that experience changed everything. It revolutionized how I viewed therapy, transformation, and my role in the healing journey. I began applying what I'd learned in new ways, trying different strategies, and adjusting the flow. Over the past decade, what started as a mentorship evolved into something I never could have imagined.

In 2017, The Intensive Method was first planted in my heart. I wanted to take the healing power of intensives—especially in the areas of trauma and addiction recovery—and make it accessible to other practitioners, no matter their specialty. I spent nearly a year building the bones of this program, and

I even wrote a proposal to present to my mentor. But just before I sent it, I had a strong sense that the timing wasn't right. So I waited. And I grieved.

I believed in this vision and I longed to share it. Colleagues would often say, "Can you teach me to do what you do?" And I wanted to say yes—but I knew I needed to honor the process.

Three years later, I became the President of Hope & Freedom.

I was fully immersed in the work offering intensives five days a week, deep in the healing trenches with clients. It wasn't until 2024 that I felt a stirring again: The Intensive Method needed to be born—not just in theory, but in form.

This time, the timing was right.

With the help of an incredible team of women, we pulled The Intensive Method online course together in just a few months. You may not know them by name, but their fingerprints are all over this course, cohorts, community, and book. Their brilliance, creativity, and heart have shaped what you've just read.

This is more than a method—it's a calling. A passion project. A purpose-driven invitation to create something that not only changes your clients' lives but transforms yours as well.

When I began, I chose Hope & Freedom because it was an out-of-the-box model. It gave me structure and confidence. But what I didn't expect was how profoundly it would affect my life—my heart, my relationships, my finances, and my faith. I've led hundreds of clients through intensives and witnessed life-changing results. If new clients could only hear from former ones, they'd know what I know: this work is powerful. It's worth the leap.

So as you finish this book, here's my encouragement to you:

Don't wait until you feel completely ready.

Don't let fear or skepticism hold you back.

Don't miss the chance to change someone's life and your own.

You have what you need to begin. You have tools, templates, and a roadmap, but more than that, you have heart, and that is what will carry this work forward. The Intensive Method isn't just about scheduling or strategy—it's about presence, passion, and purpose.

If you've been considering joining an online cohort or our TIM community, I'd encourage you to take that next step. Having someone walk alongside you—like my mentor did for me—can make all the difference. Visit theintensivemethod.com to explore all of the available resources and pathways to greater connection and community.

People are hurting. They're looking for clarity, for hope, and for healing, and they're willing to invest in someone who can offer a complete and compassionate path forward.

You can be that person.

This method empowers you, but it also empowers your clients. It gives you a business you can sustain, a life you can enjoy, and work that leaves a legacy of transformation.

So take what you've learned, use it with courage, and go build a life and business you love.

Because when you thrive, your clients thrive too.

—Tina

Ready to Take the Next Step?

This book is meant to be practical, but it's also meant to be lived out. If *Integrating The Intensive Method* sparked ideas, clarity, or conviction, here are a few ways to keep moving forward in a way that fits your pace, goals, and practice.

Access the Resources

Many of the tools referenced in this book—worksheets, planning guides, templates, and implementation resources—are available for purchase and download online.

These resources are designed to help you move from concept to structure with clarity and confidence.

Visit: theintensivemethod.com/resources

Learn at Your Own Pace

If you want guided, self-paced learning with reflection prompts, worksheets, and step-by-step structure, the **The Intensive Method Online Course** walks you through the full process of designing, refining, and implementing your intensive offering.

This option is ideal if you want depth, flexibility, and a clear framework you can return to as your practice evolves.

Learn more: theintensivemethod.com/intensive-course

Develop with Support

If you're looking for accountability, encouragement, and personalized feedback, **group coaching** offers the opportunity to develop your intensive alongside other practitioners.

This option is best for those who want support applying the method to their specific niche, practice model, and season of life.

Explore group coaching: theintensivemethod.com/coaching

However you choose to continue, my hope is that you build an intensive practice that serves your clients well *and* sustains you for the long haul.

— Tina

www.ingramcontent.com/pod-product-compliance
Lightning Source LLC
LaVergne TN
LVHW010647110826
845149LV00014B/2981